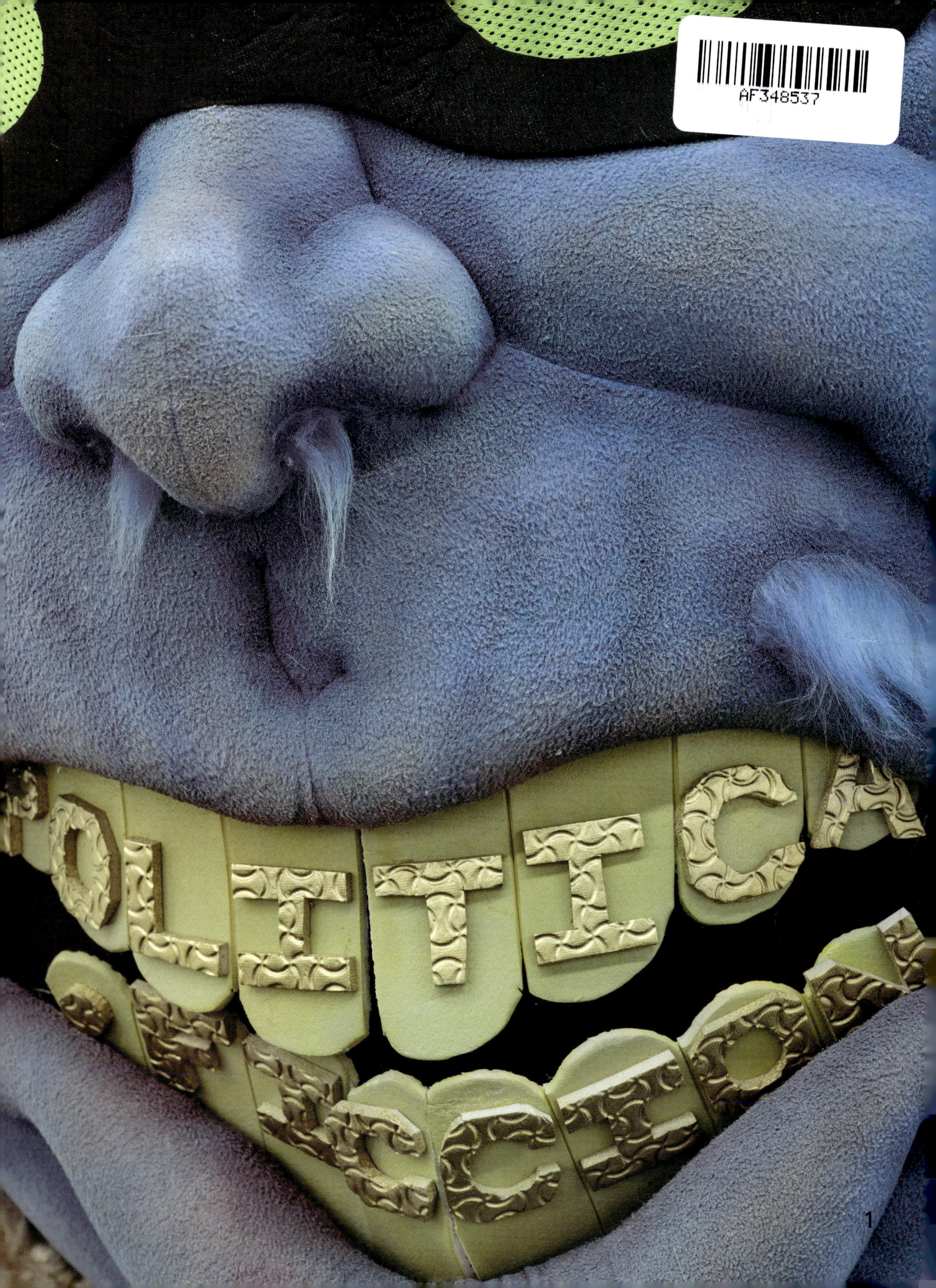

1

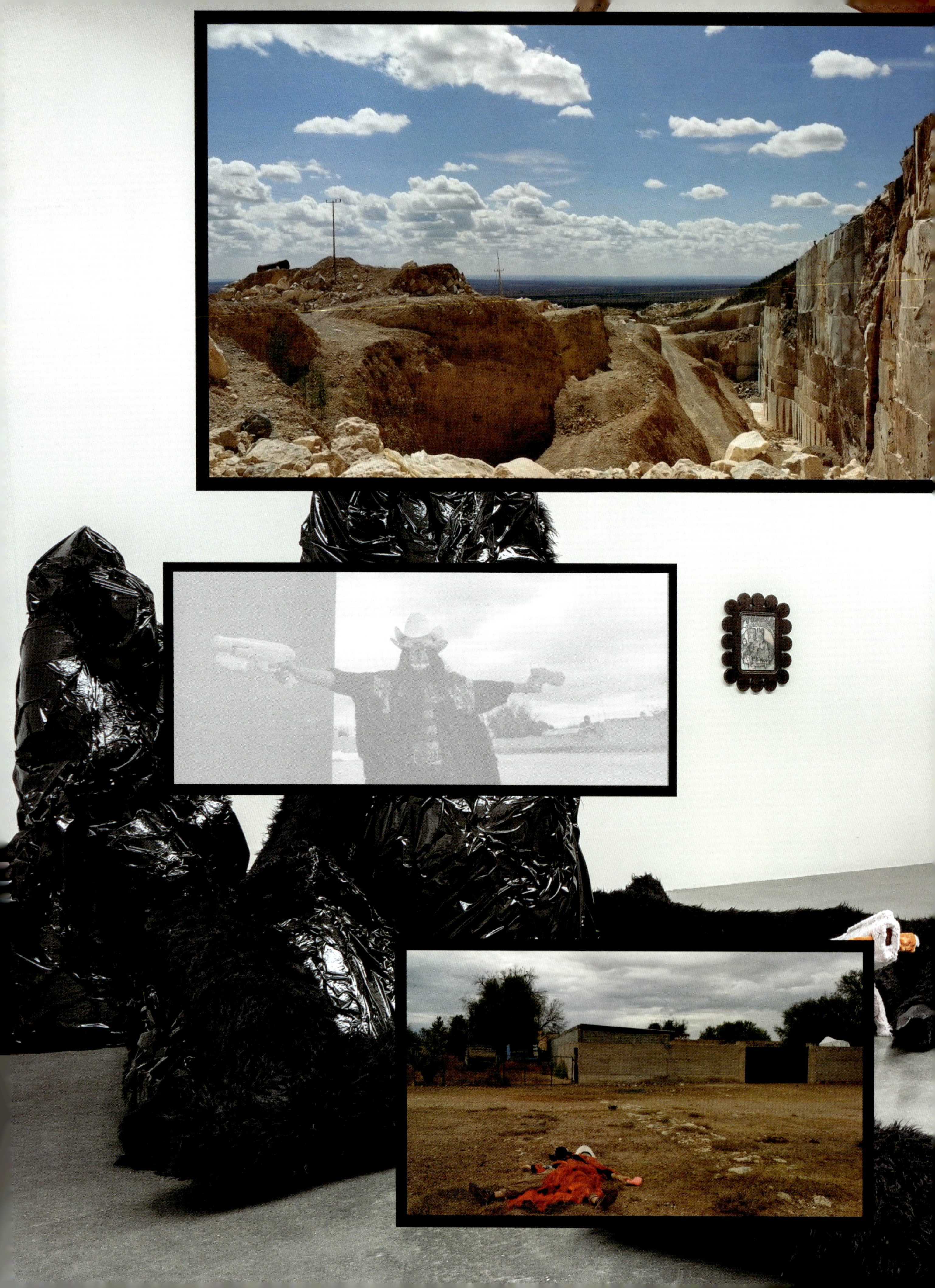

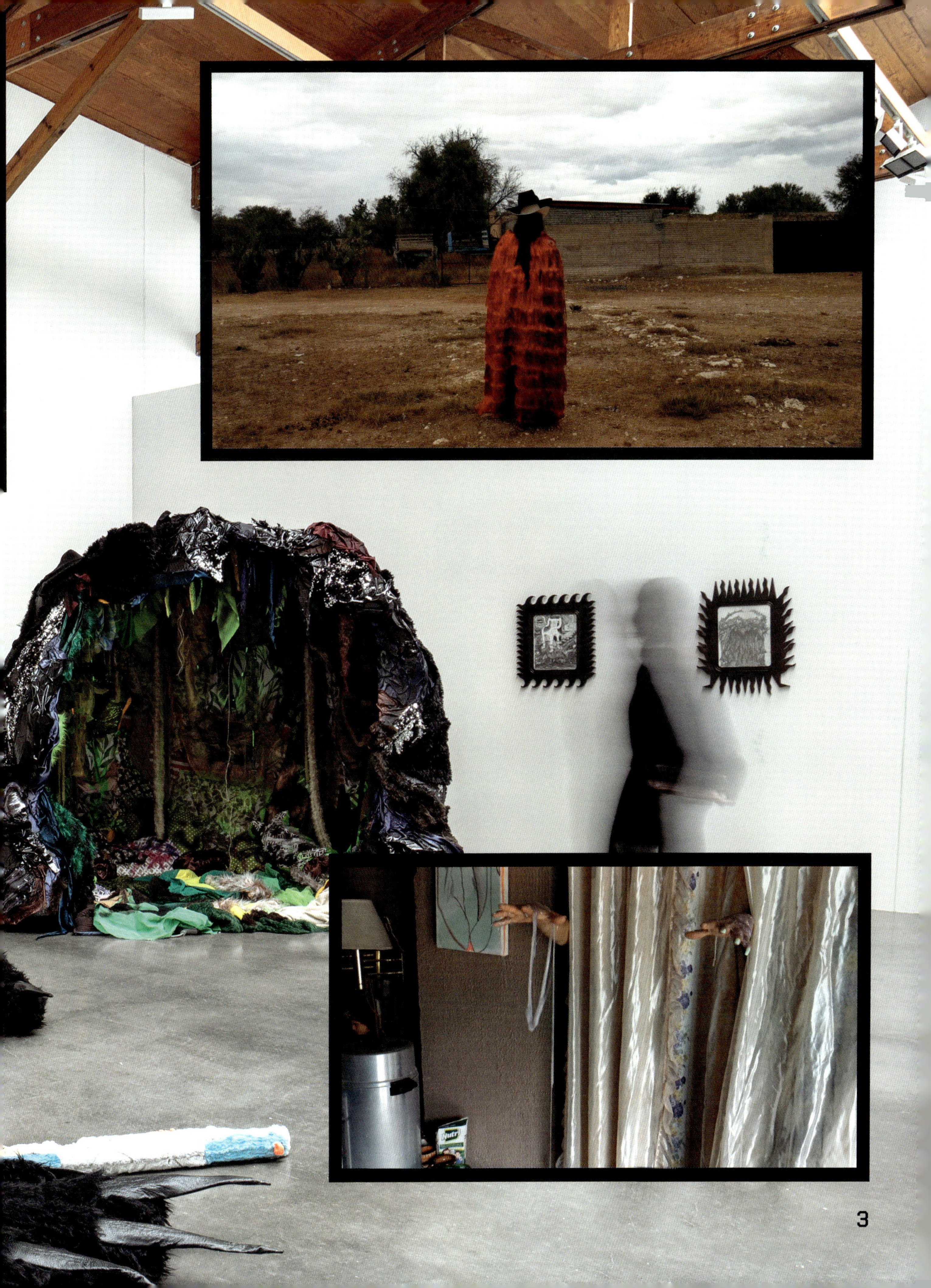

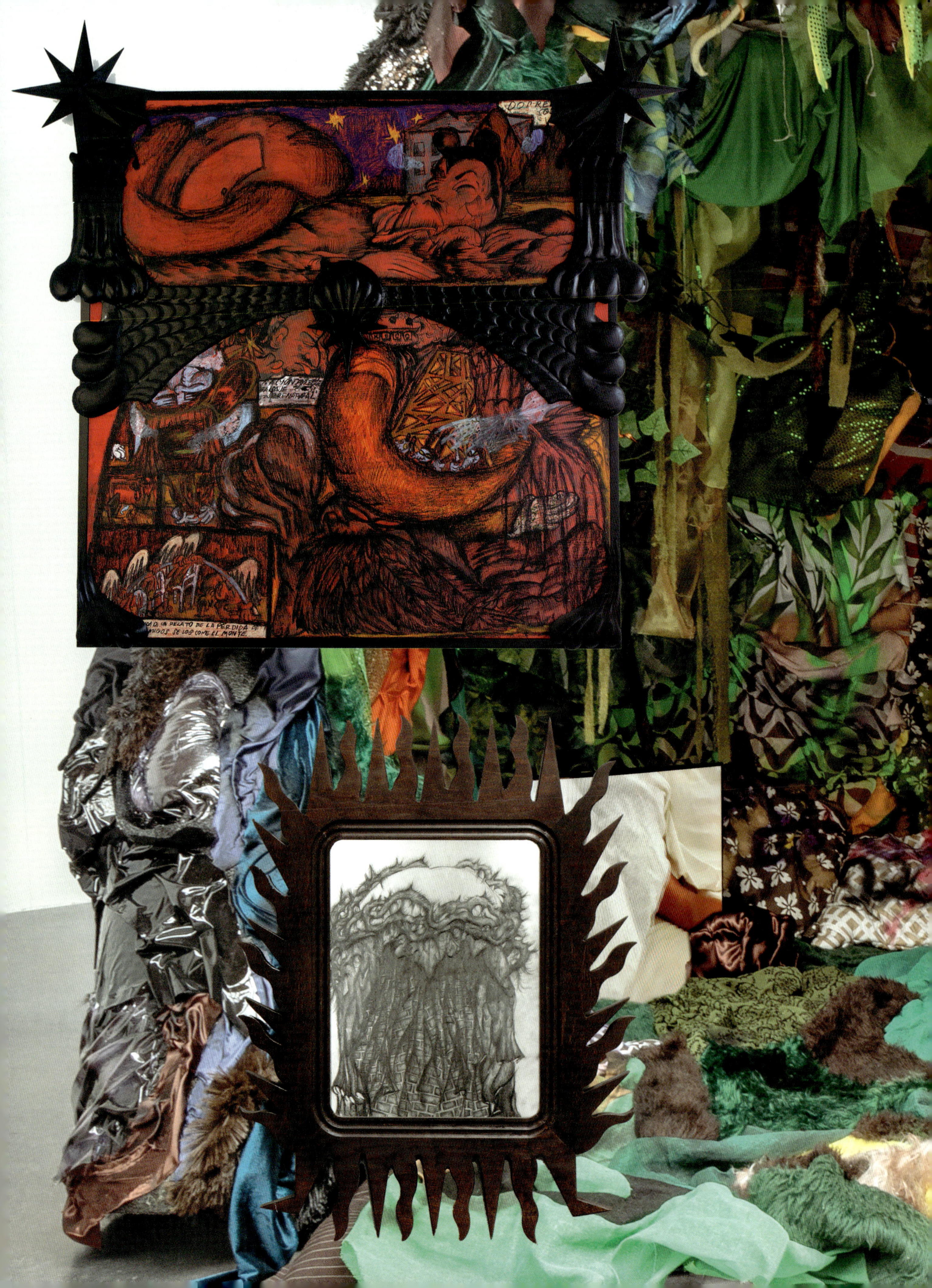

DON RE
...DO, UN RELATO DE LA PERDIDA DE
...NGOS SE LOS COME EL MONTE.

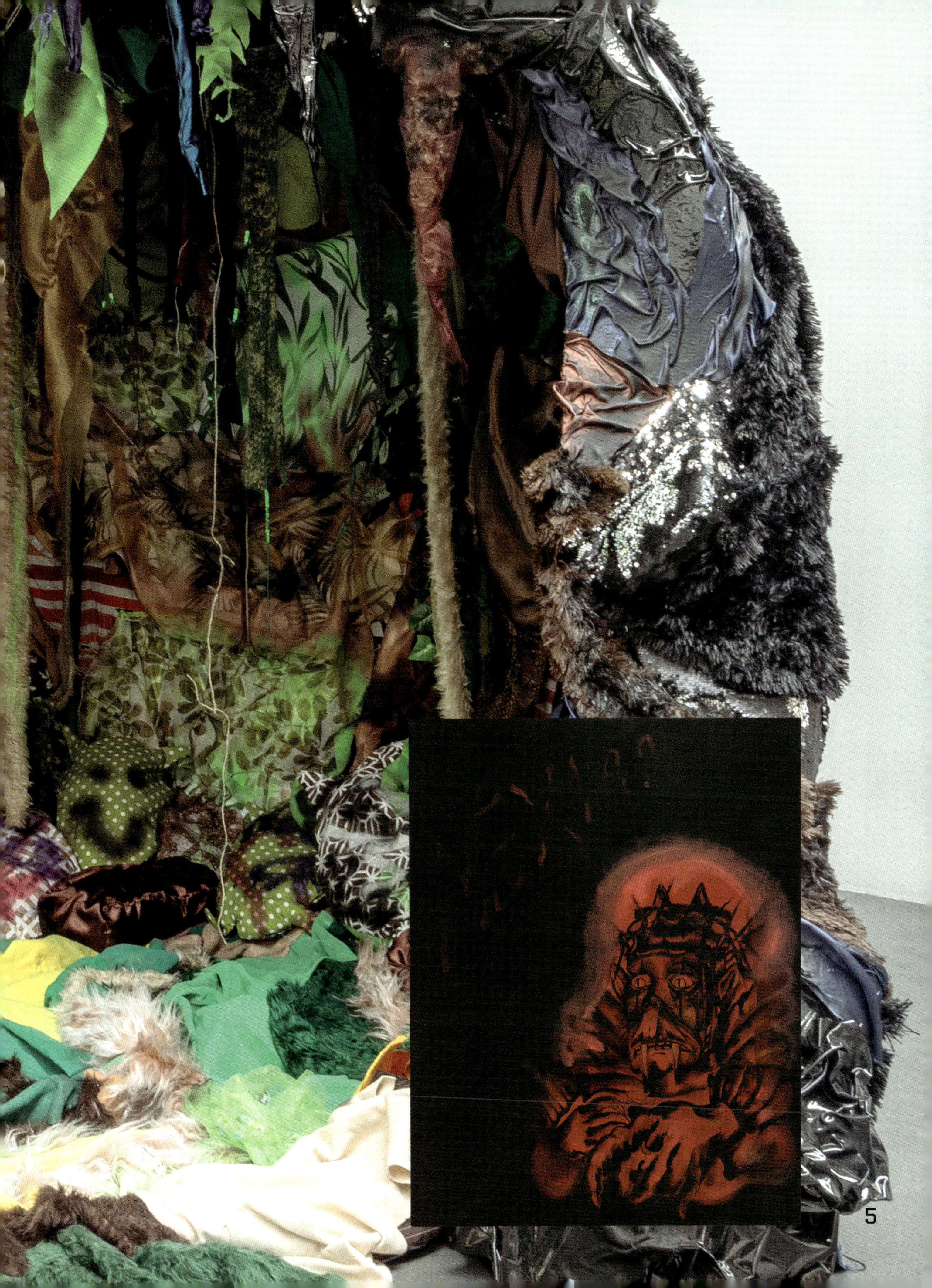

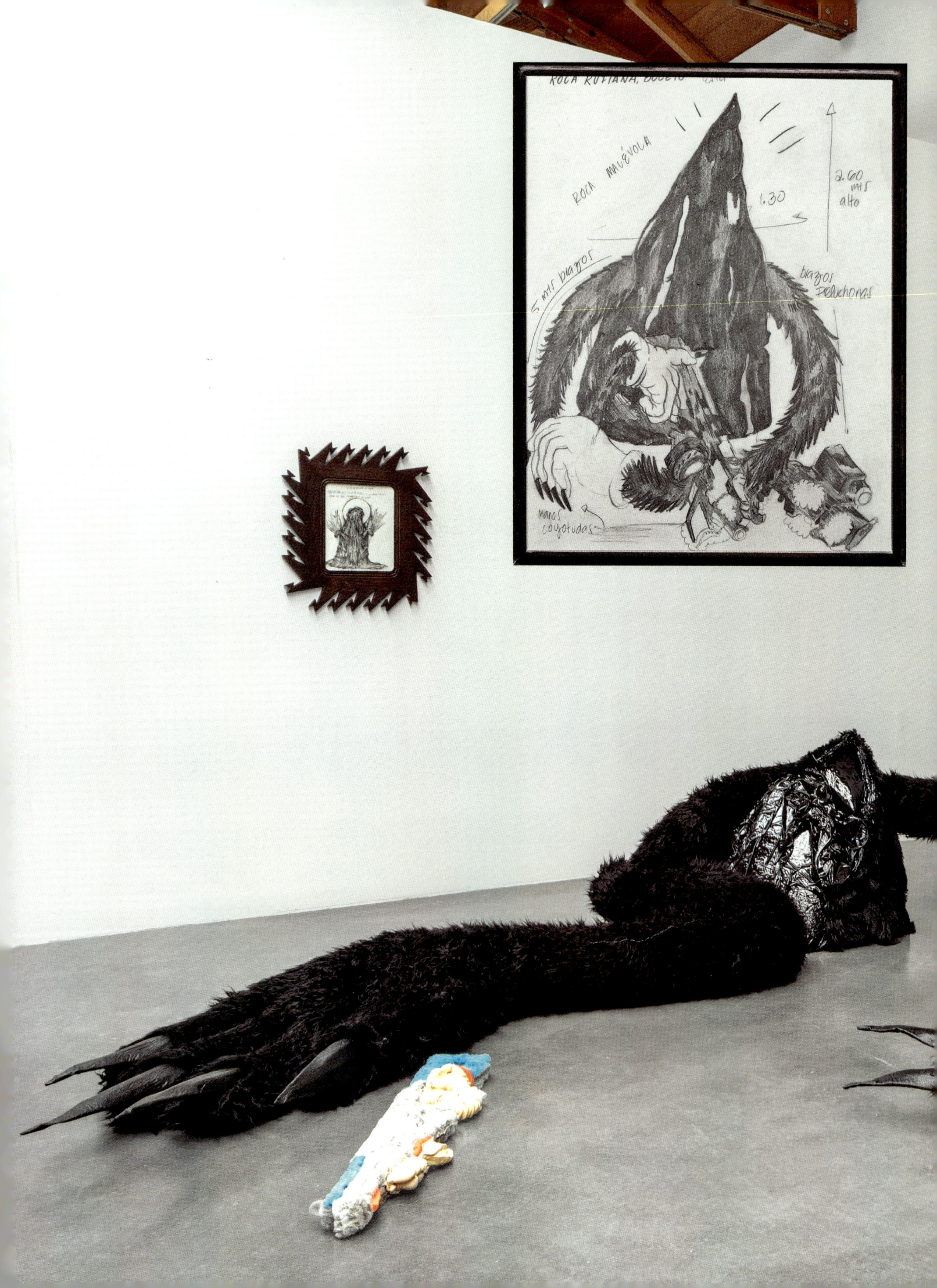

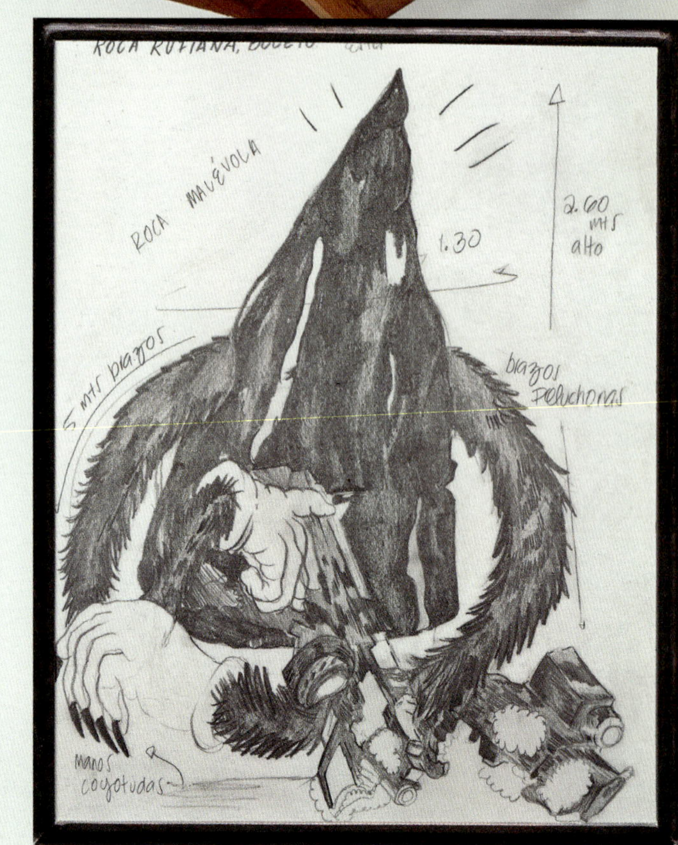

ROCA RUFIANA, BOCETO
ROCA MALÉVOLA
1.30
2.60 mts alto
5 mts brazos
brazos peluchonas
manos coyotudas

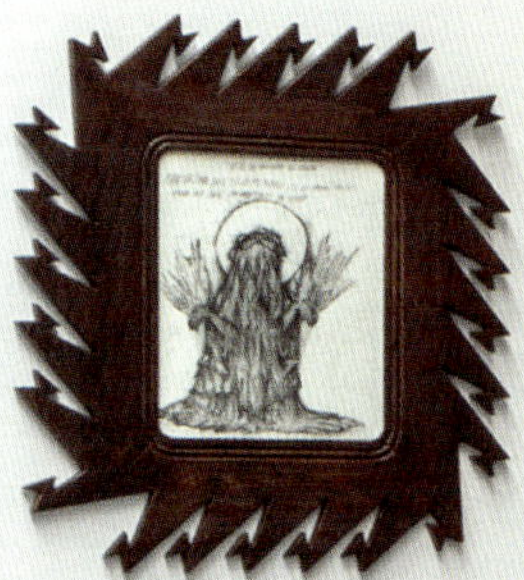

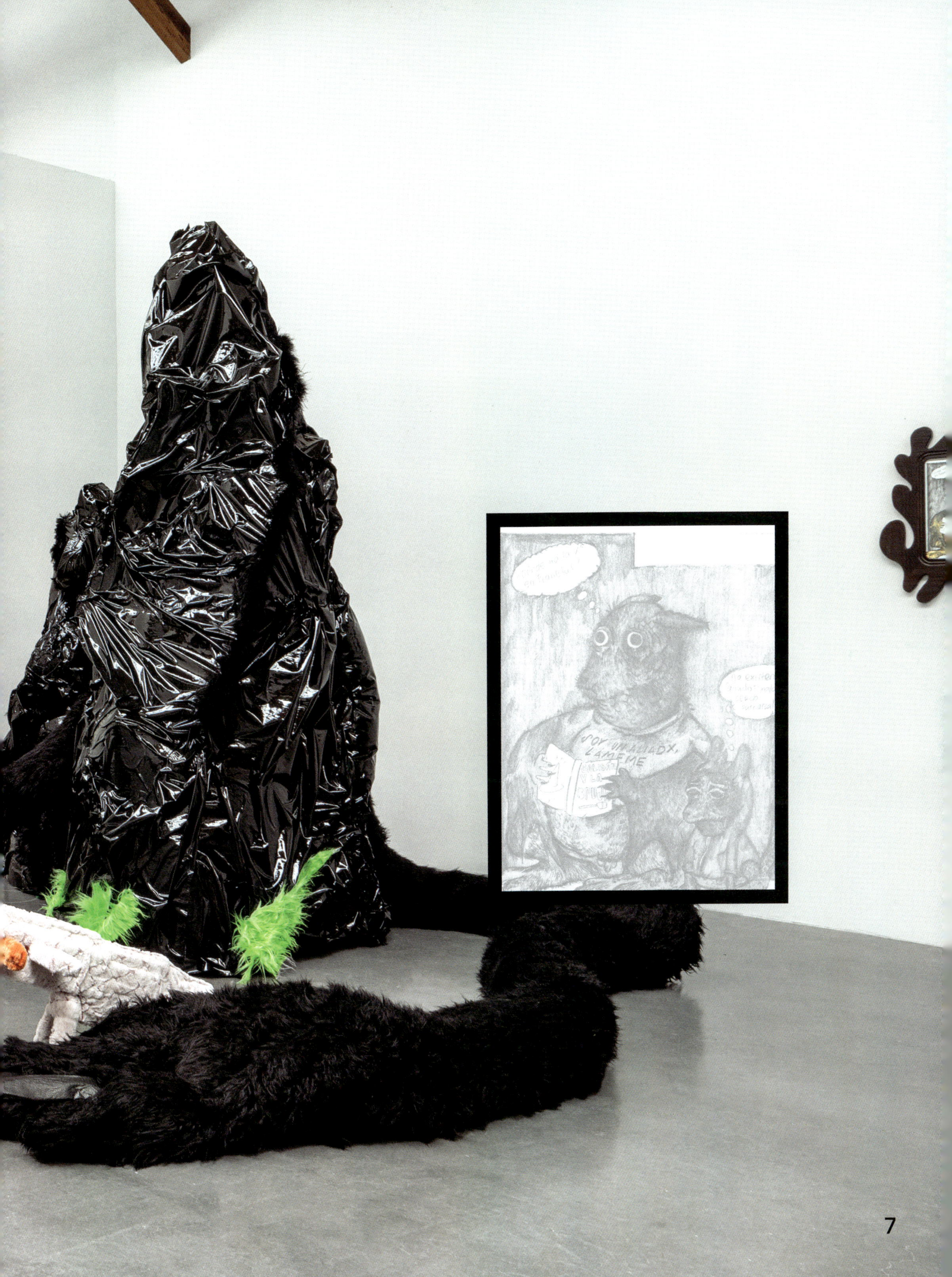

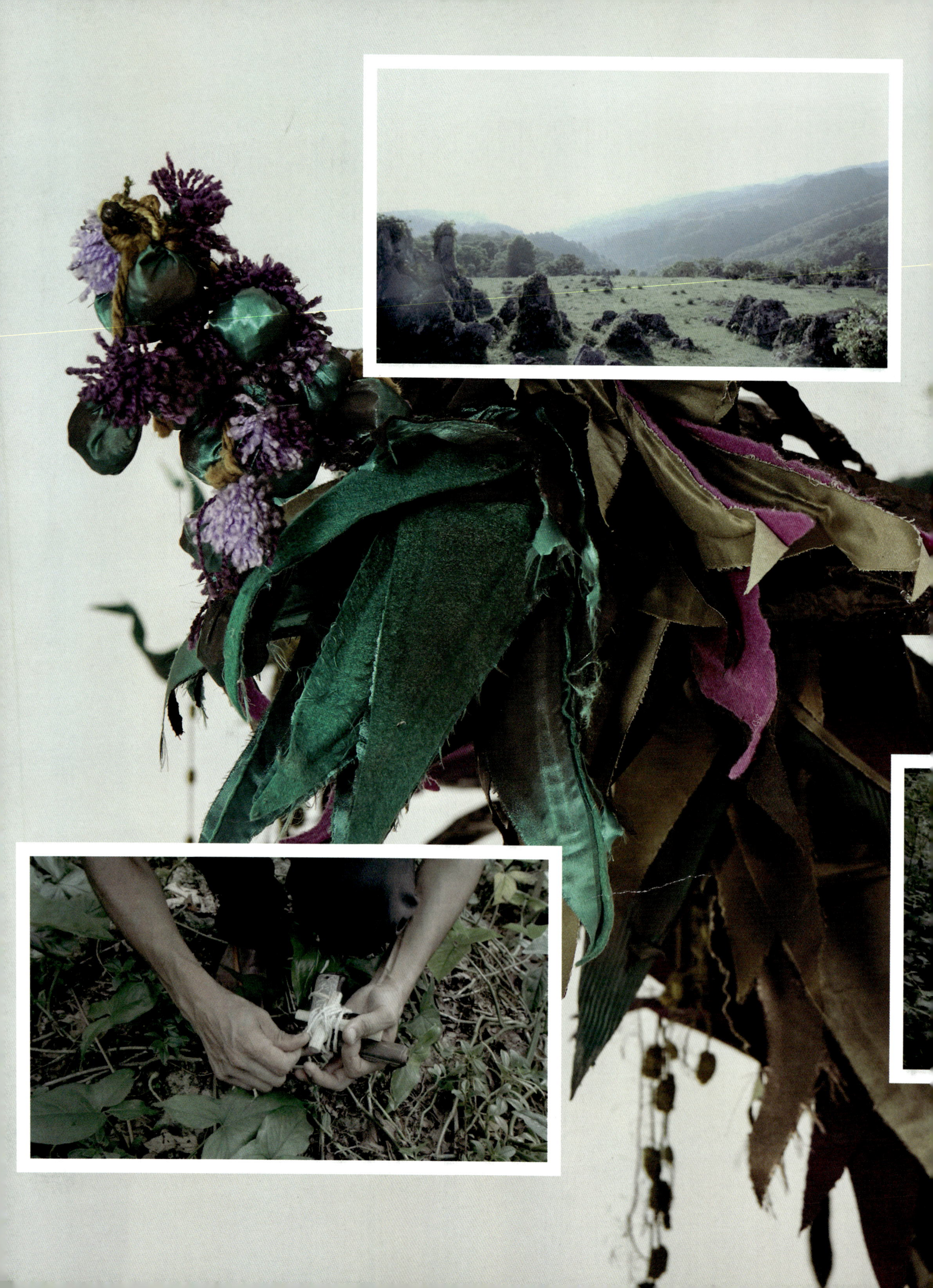

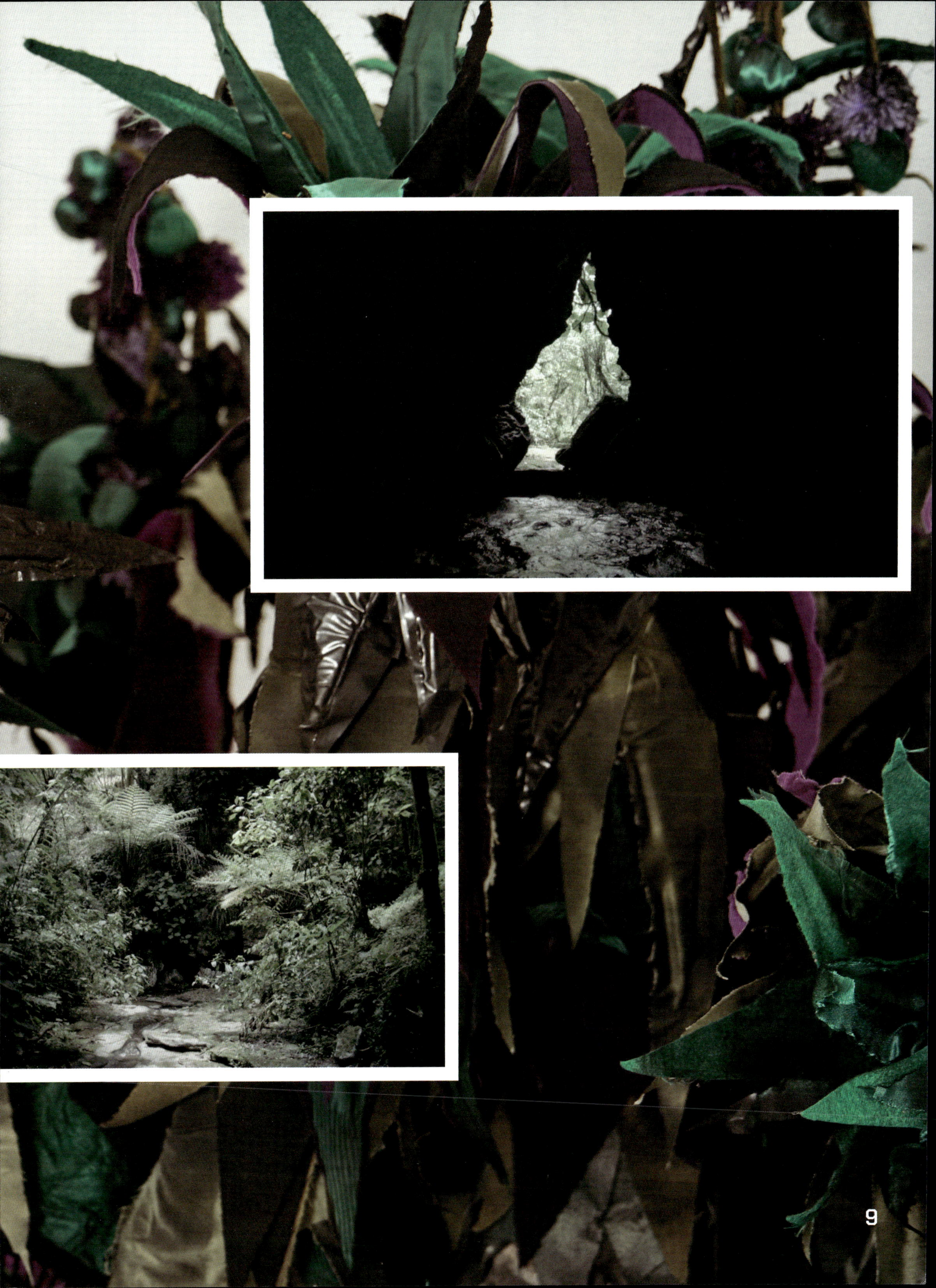

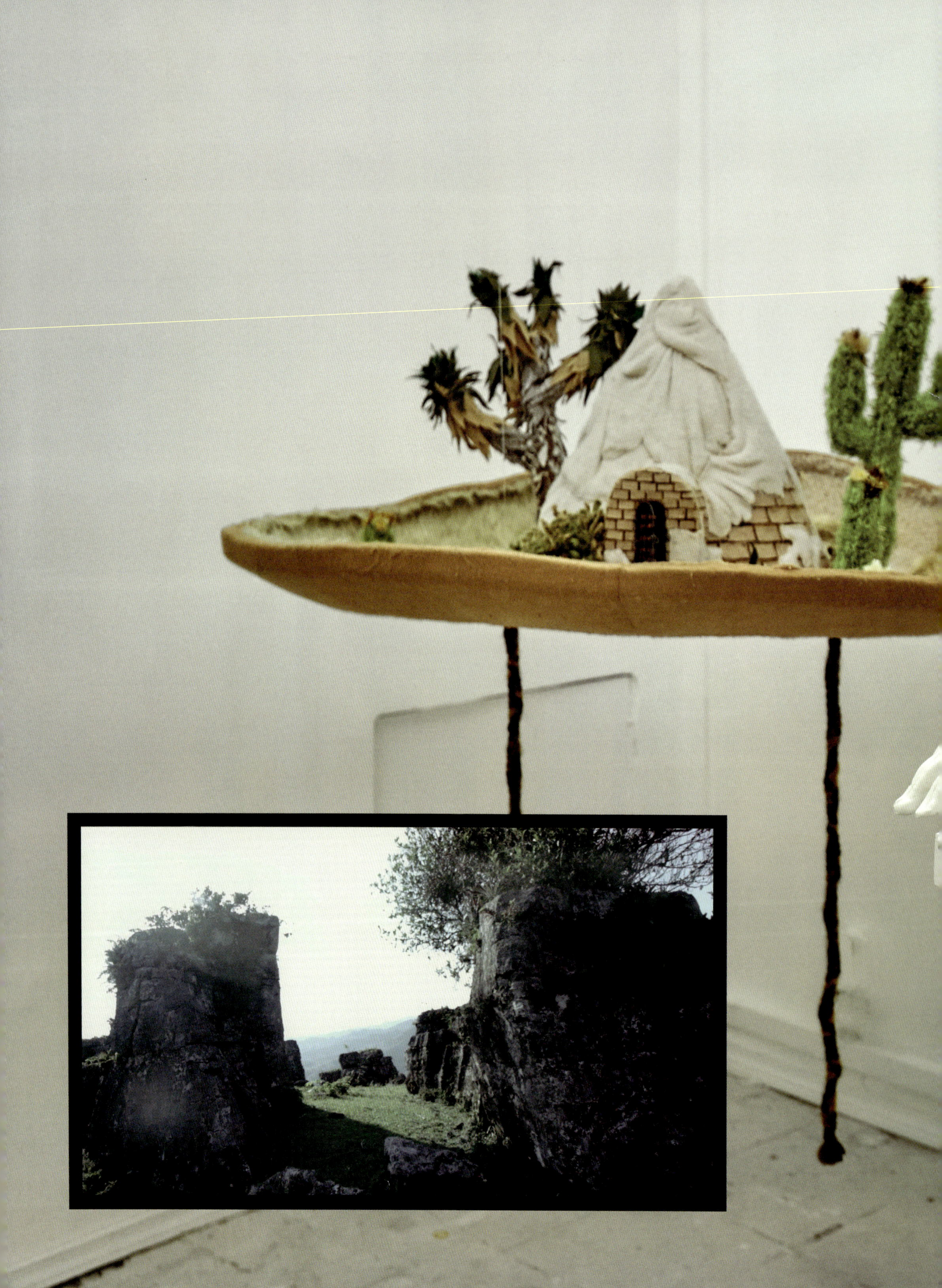

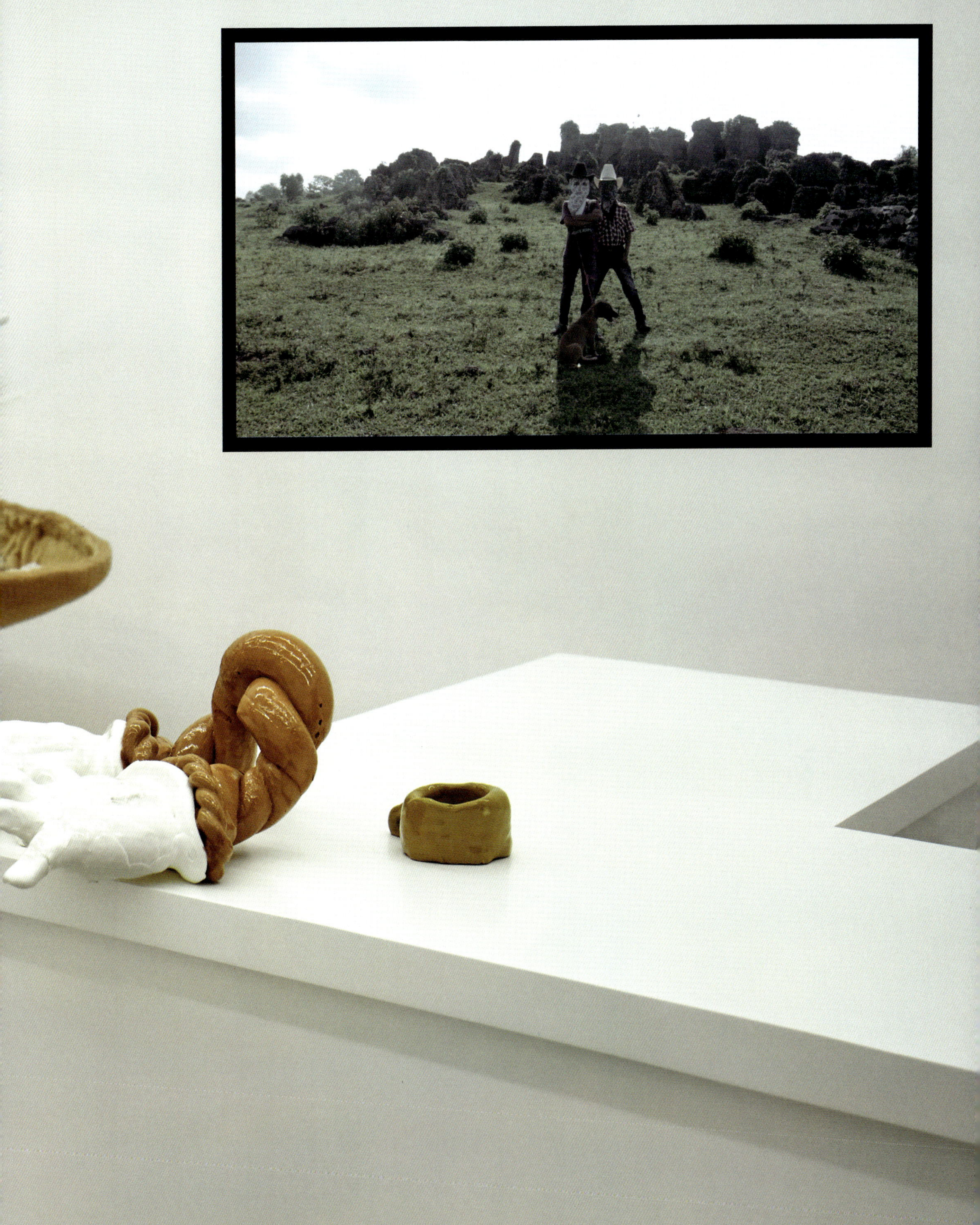

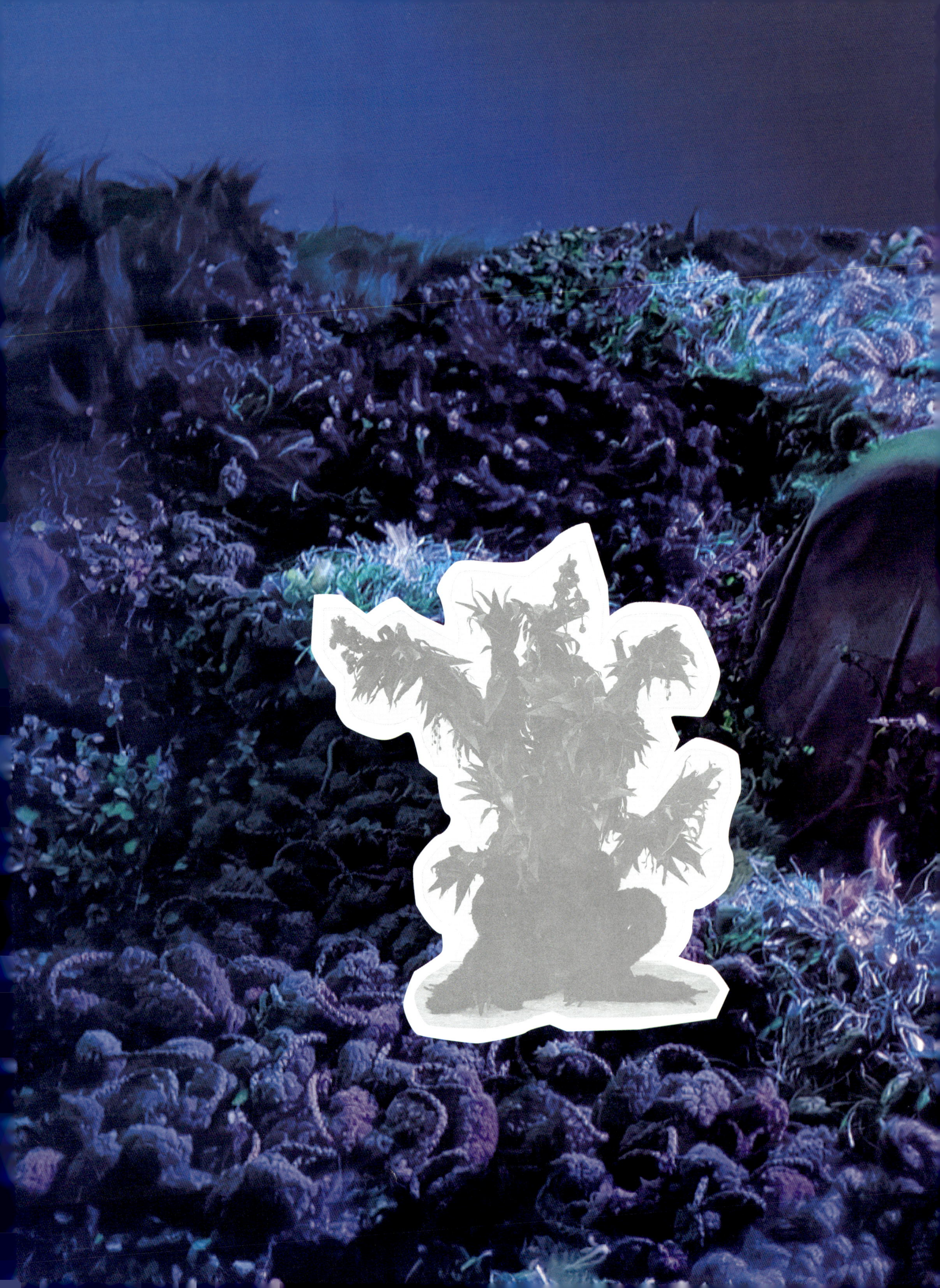

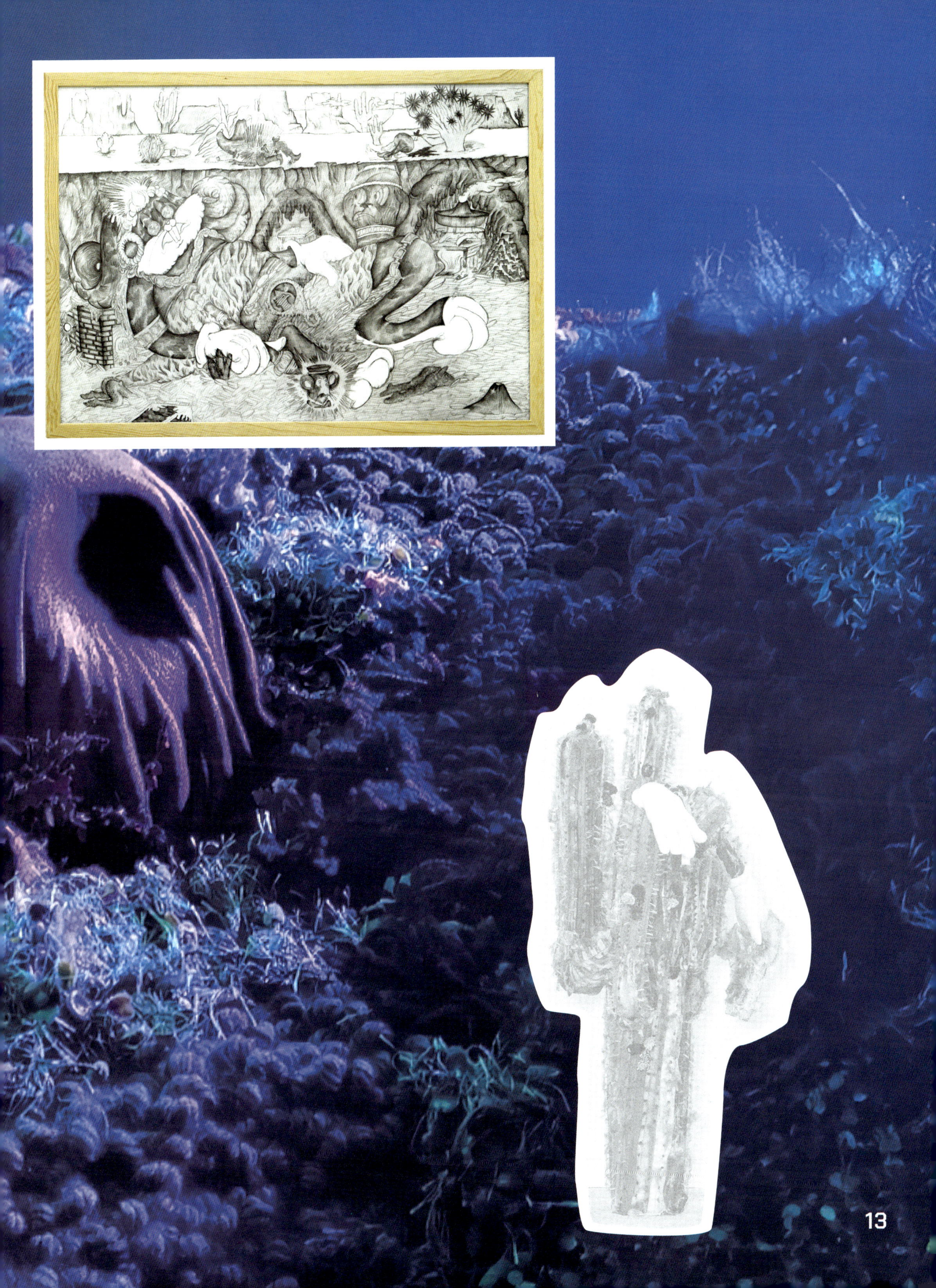

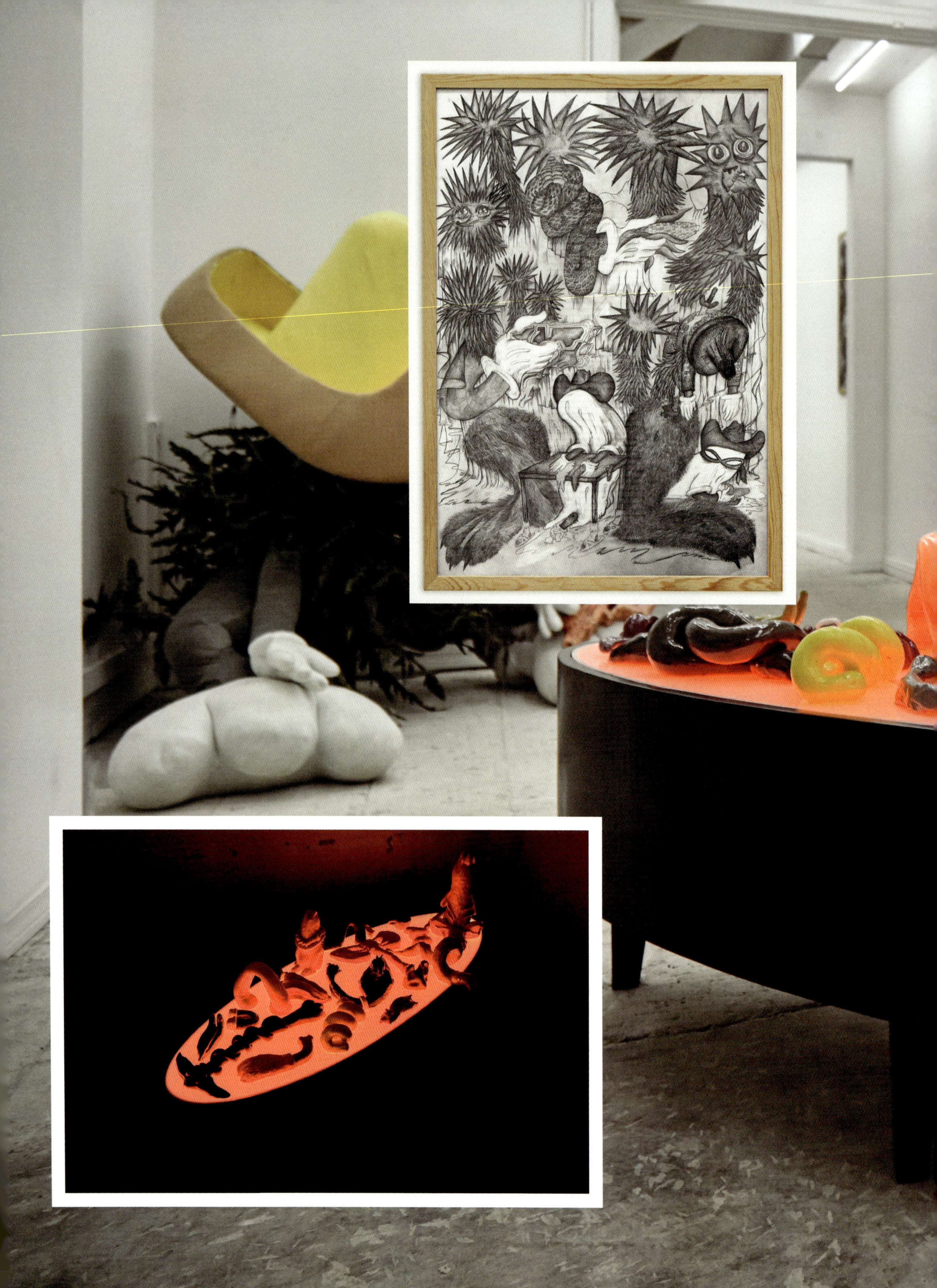

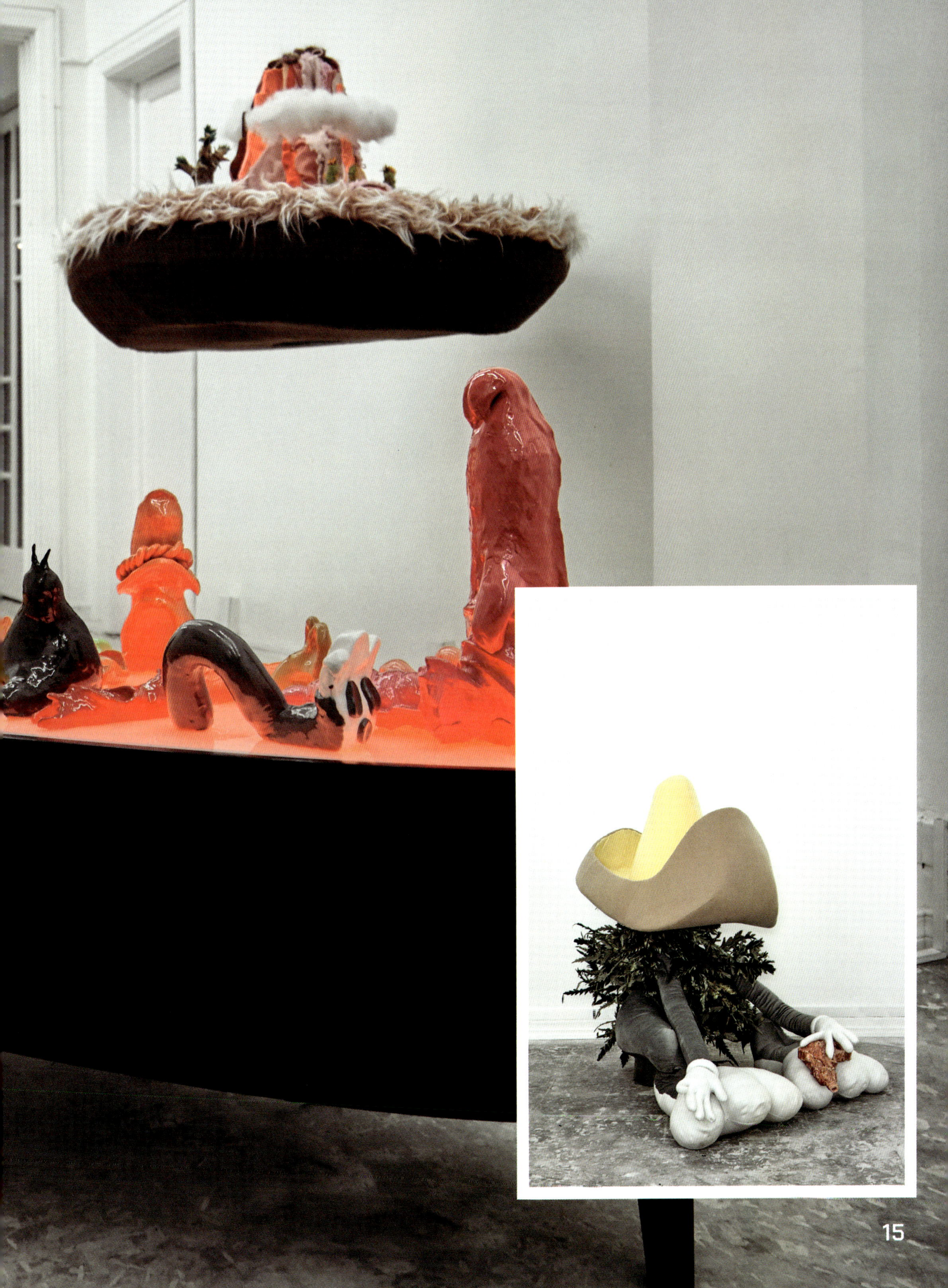

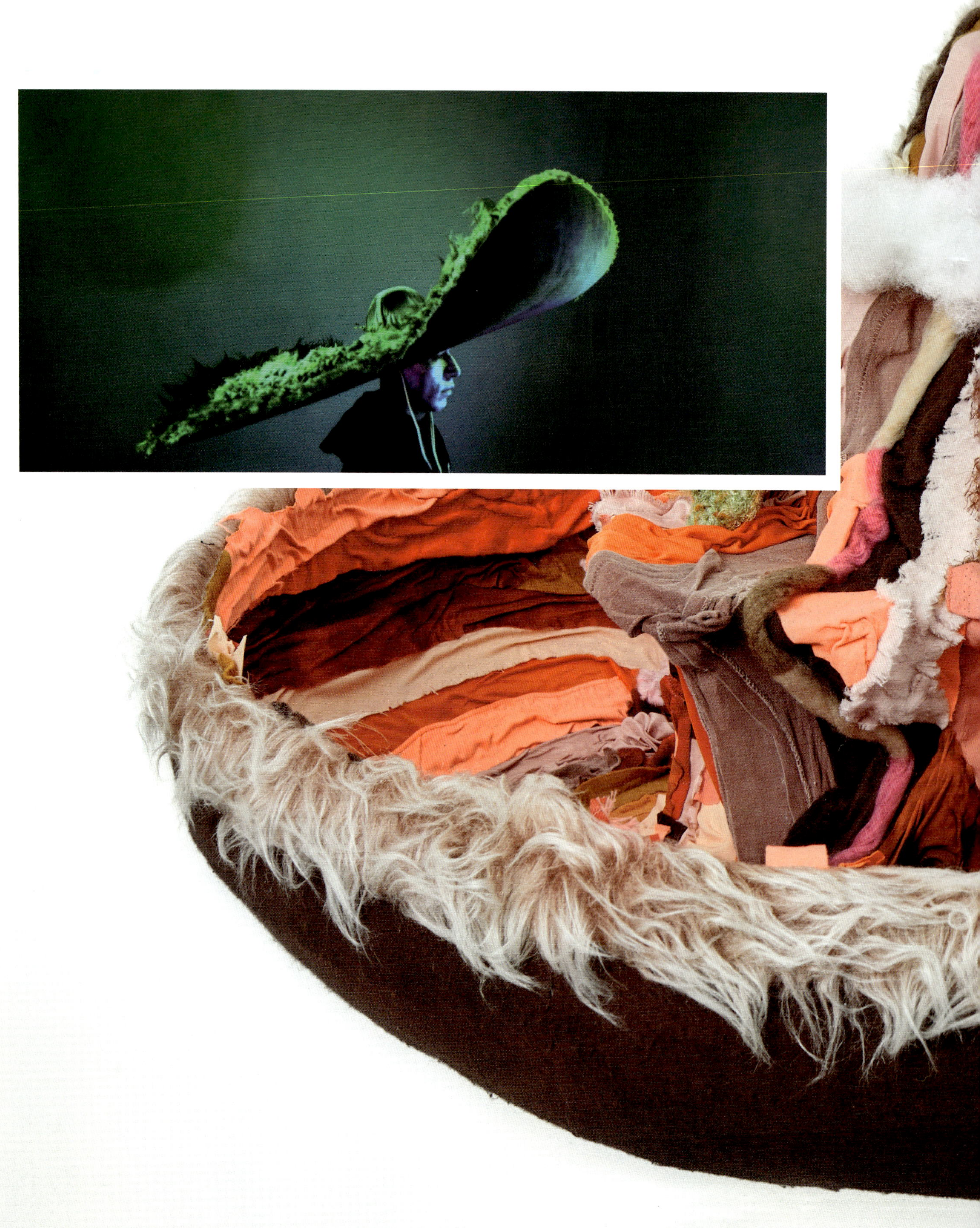

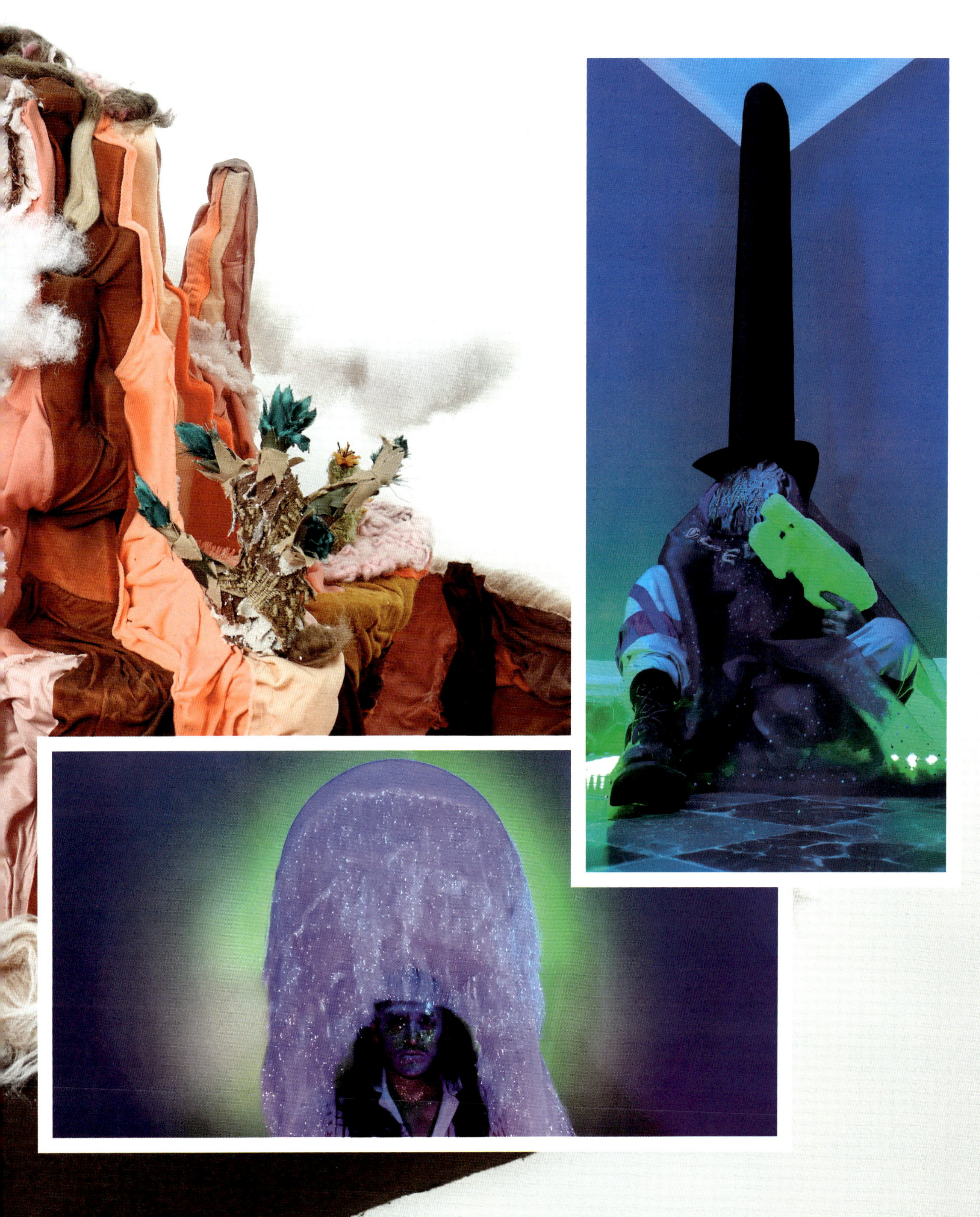

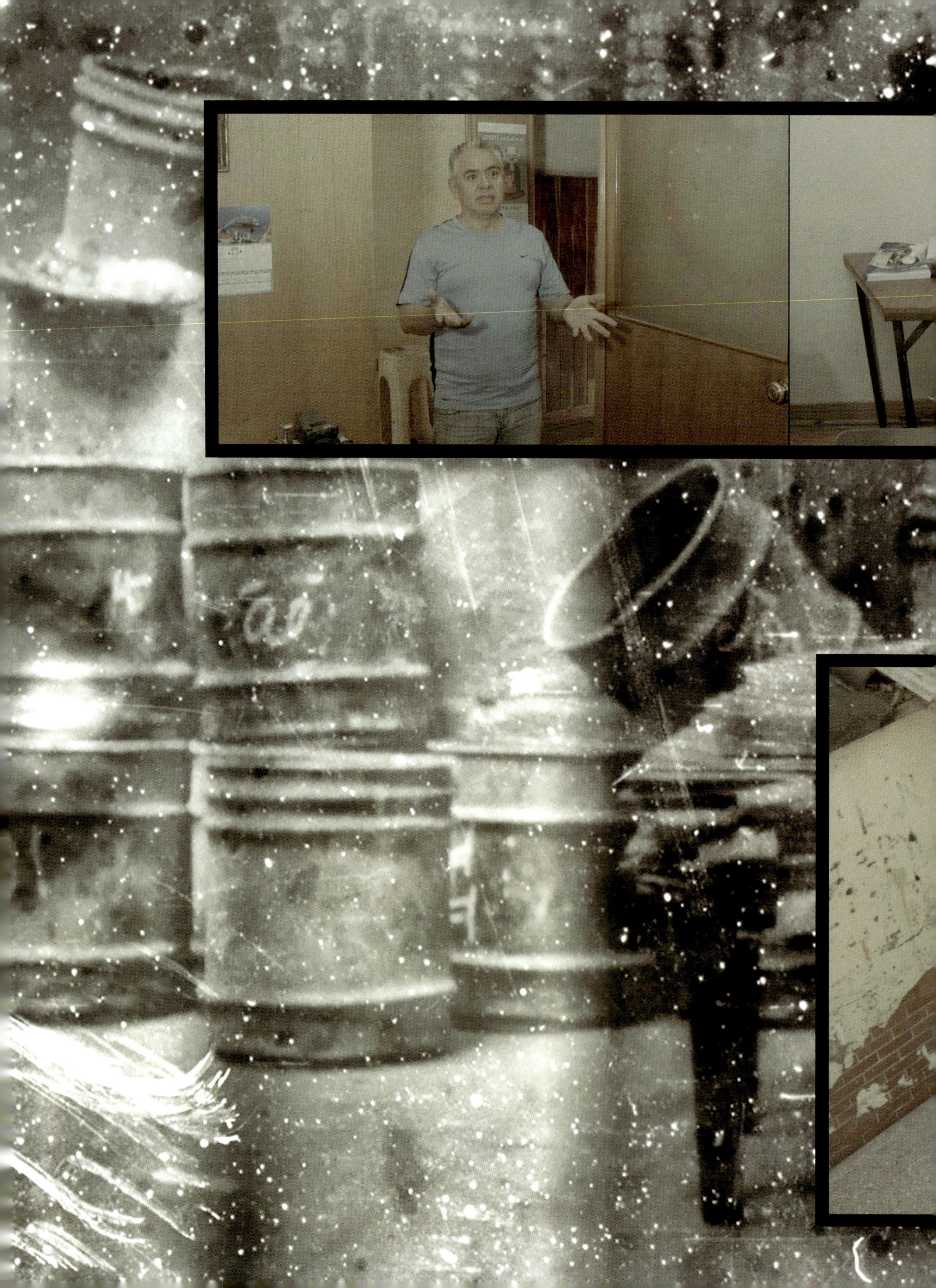

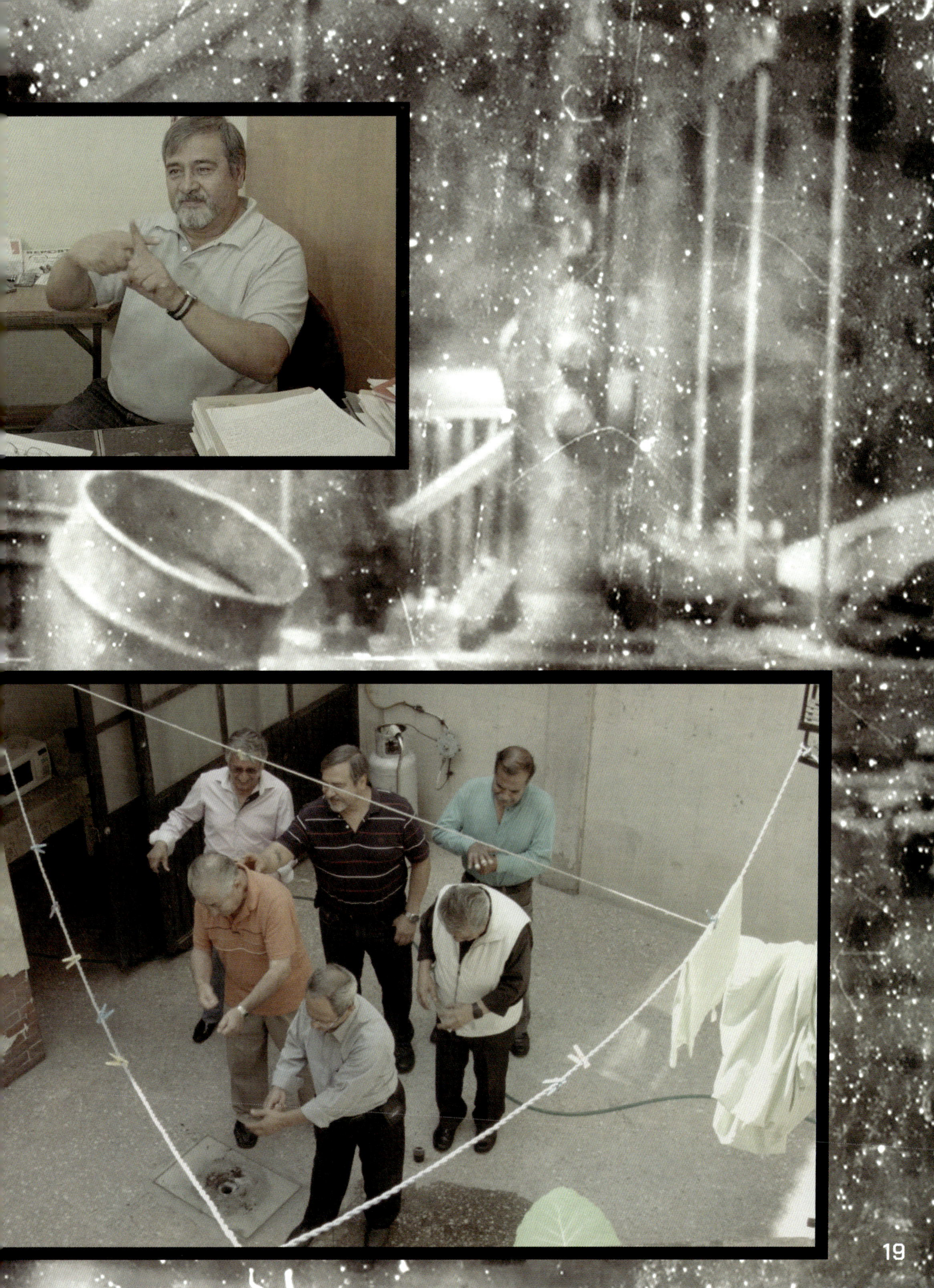

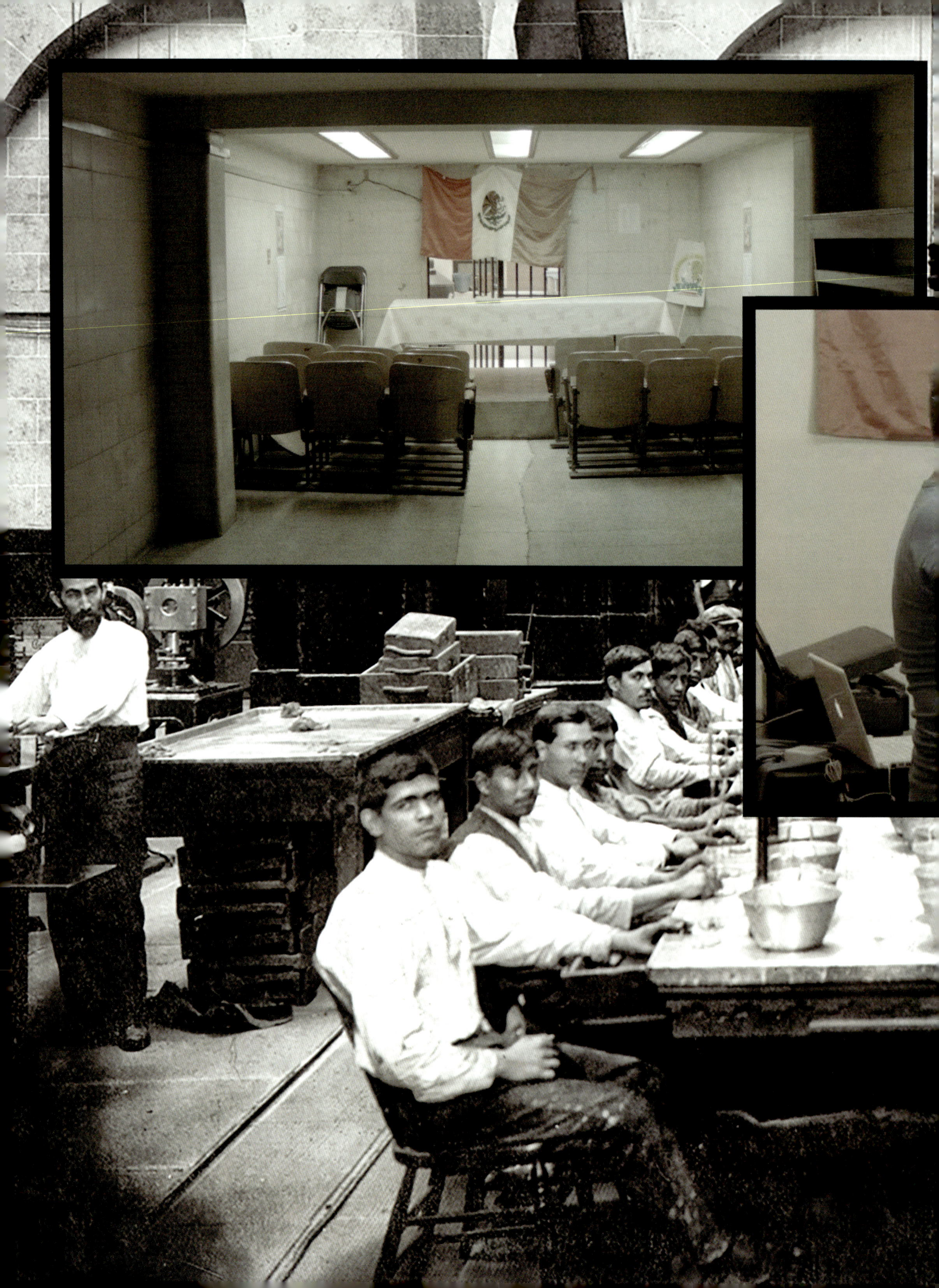

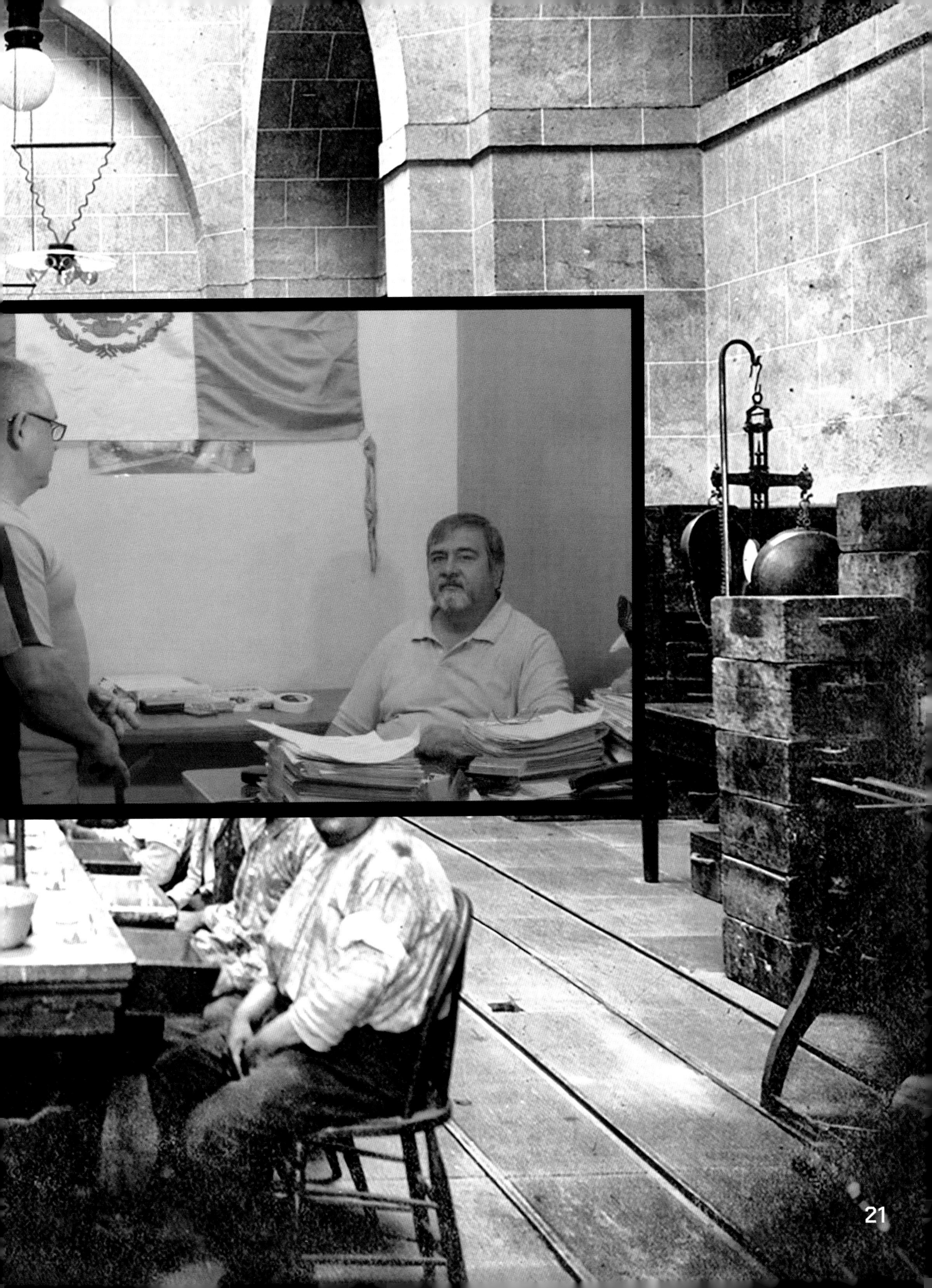

LA FIEBRE DE ORO

UNA PELÍCULA DE PALOMA CONTRERAS LOMAS

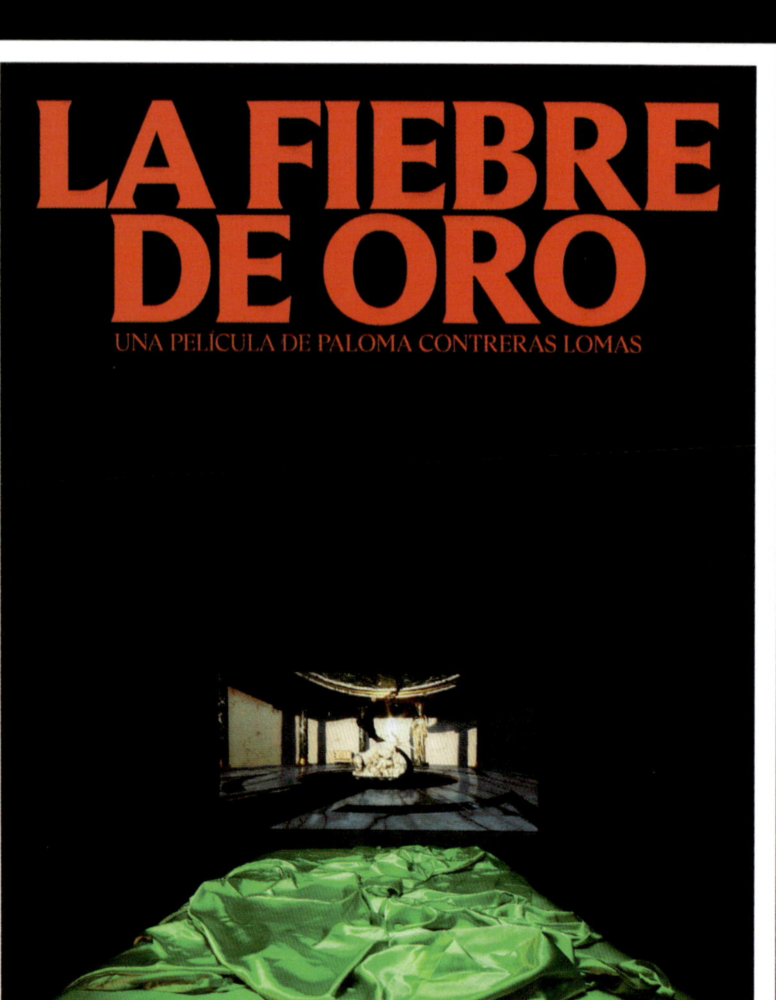

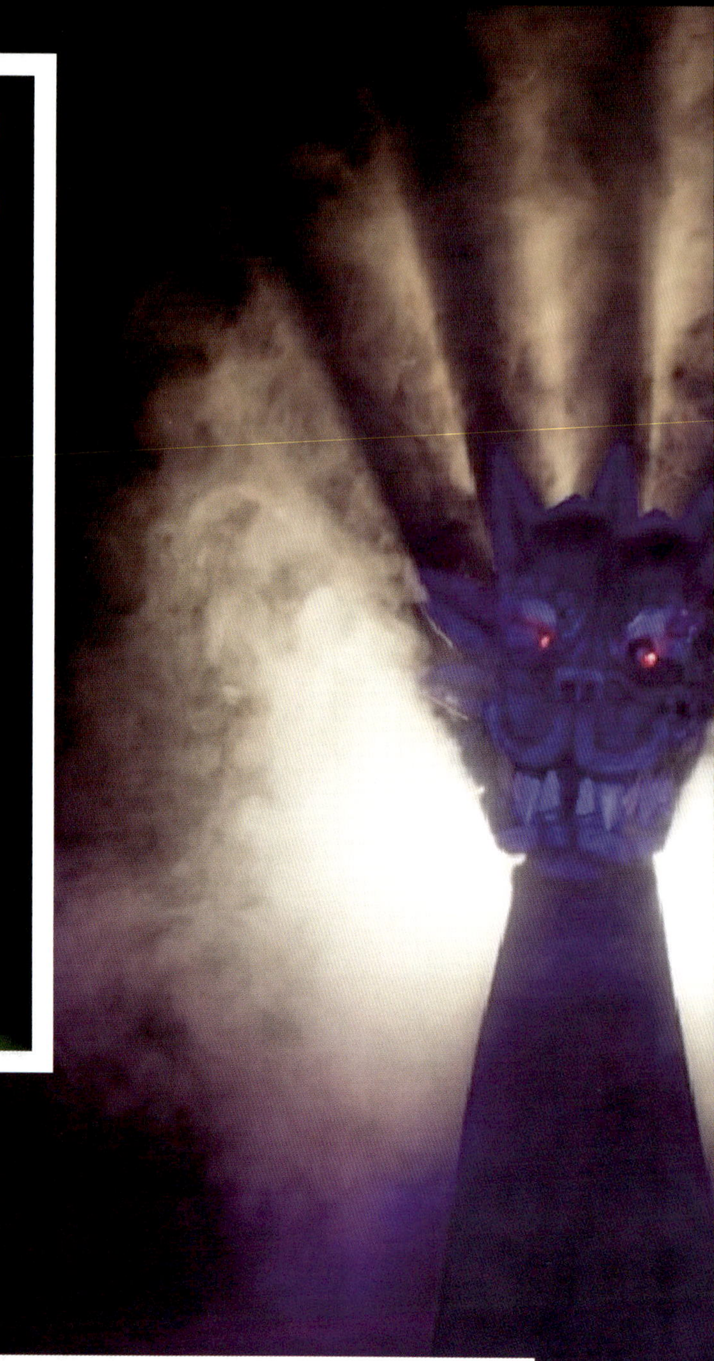

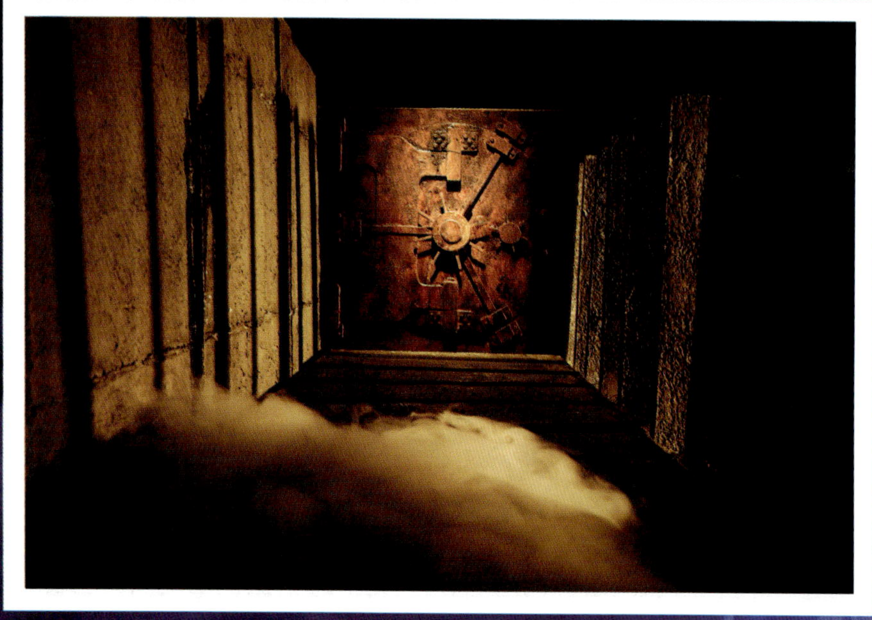

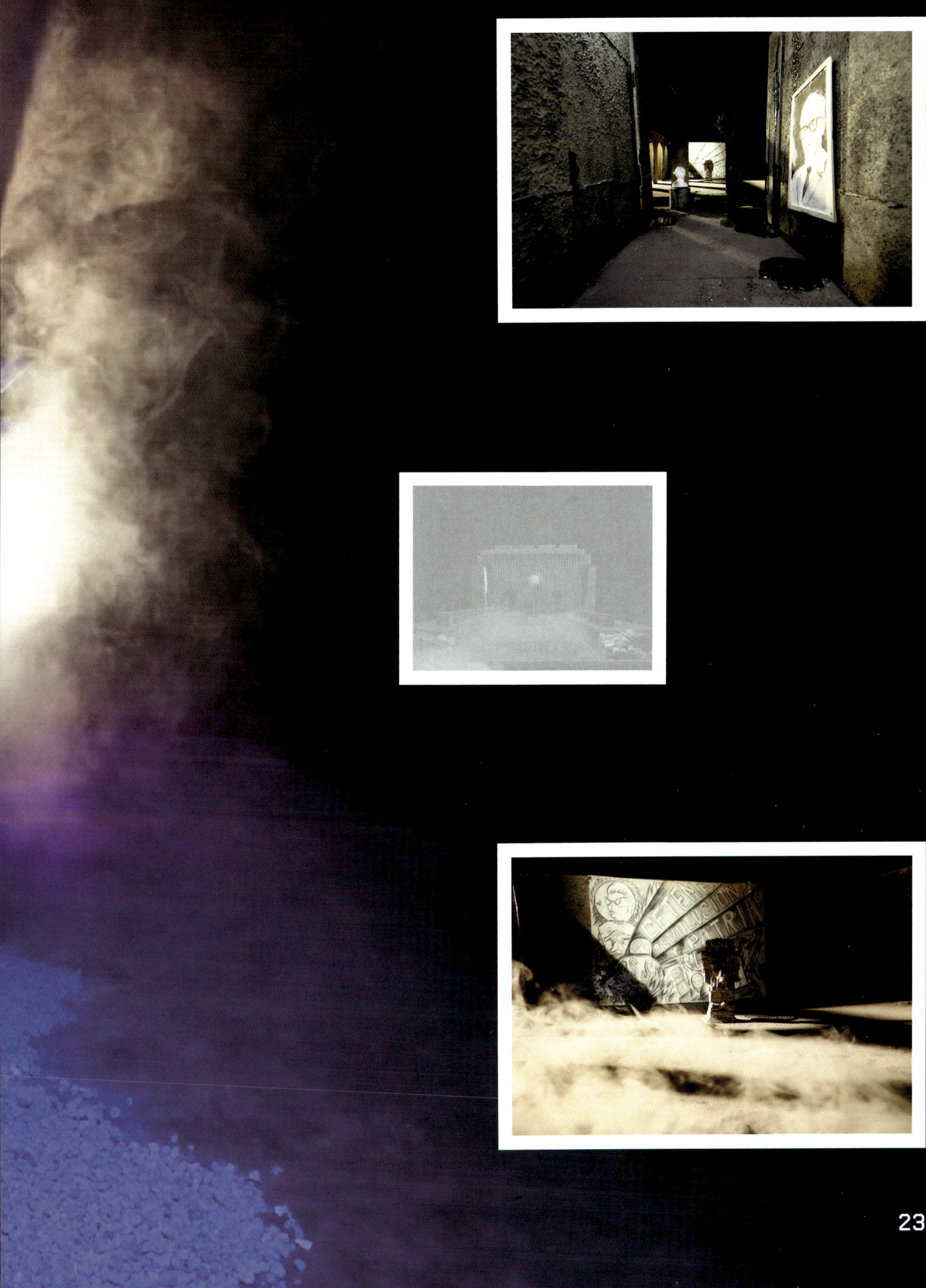

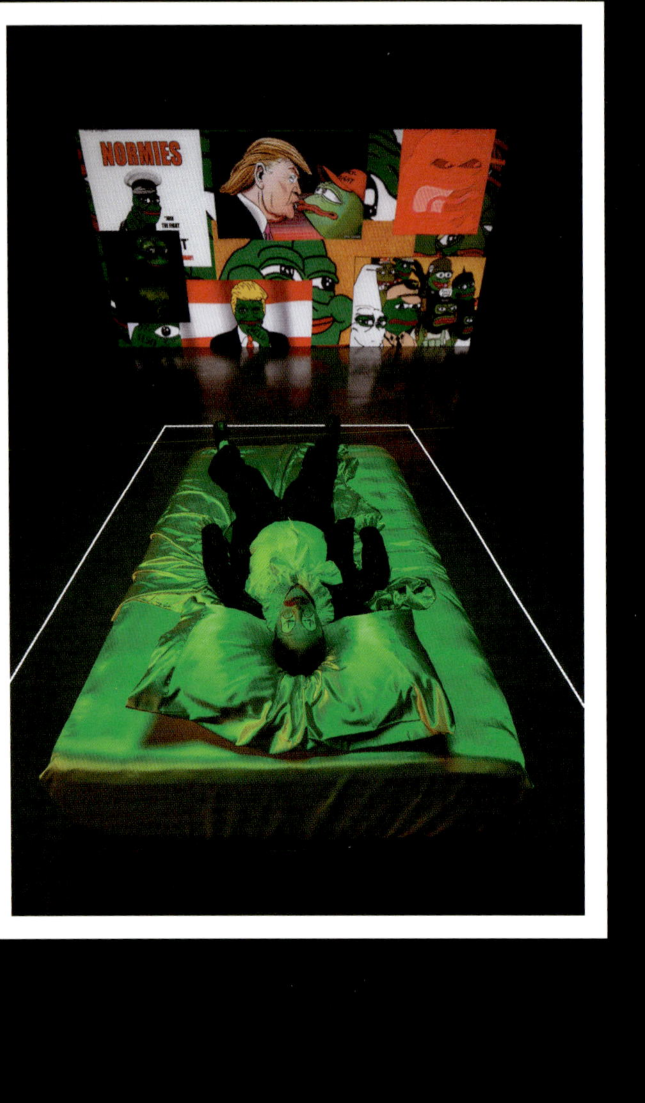
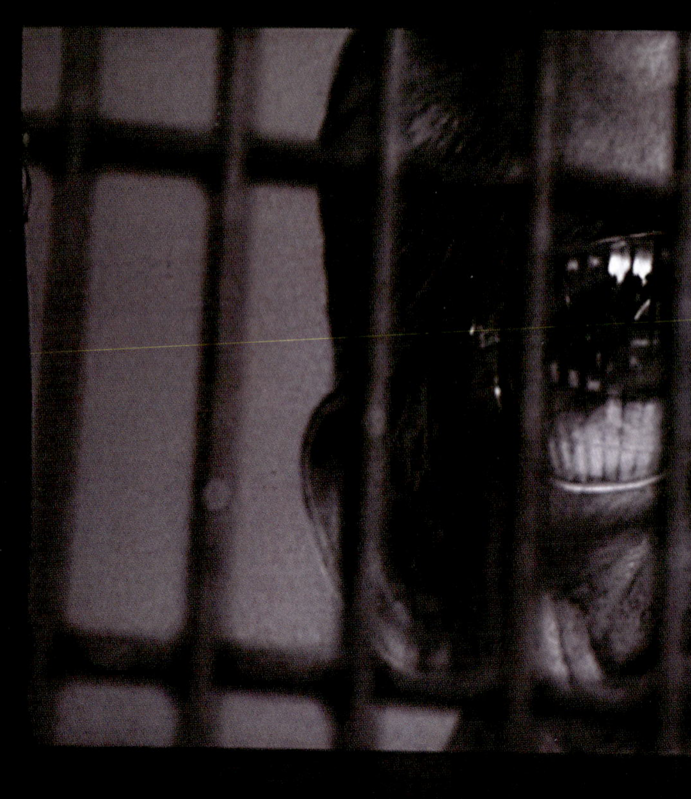
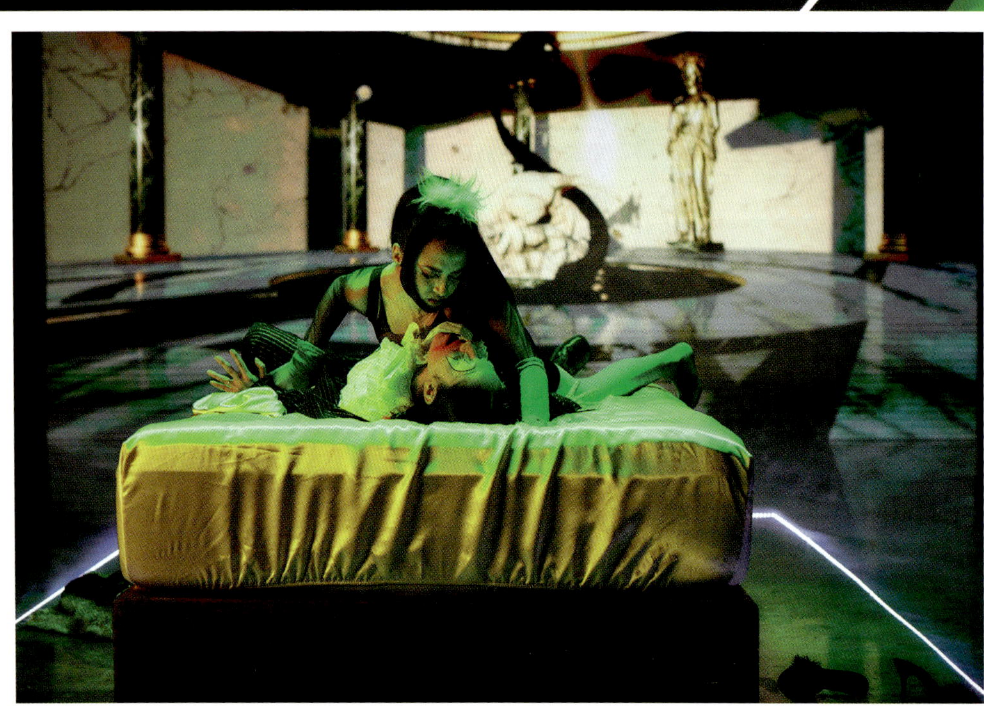

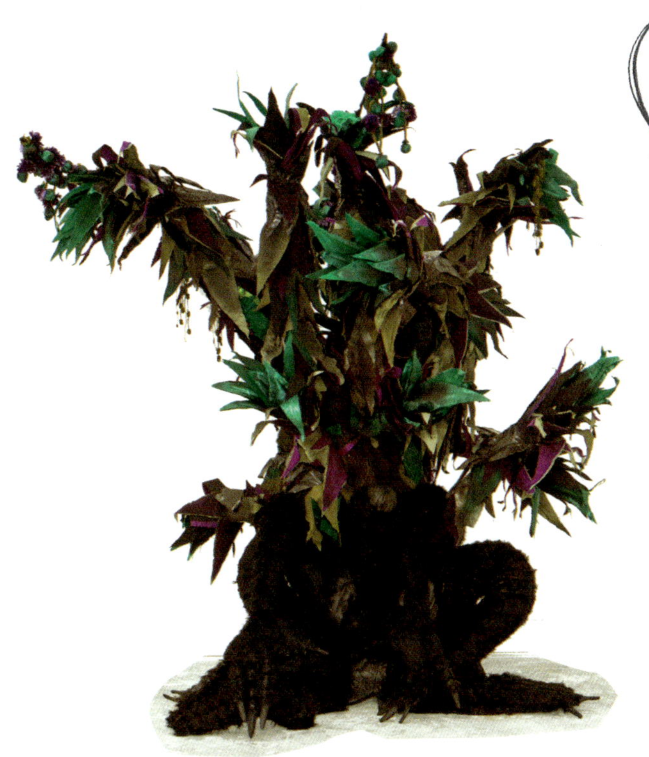
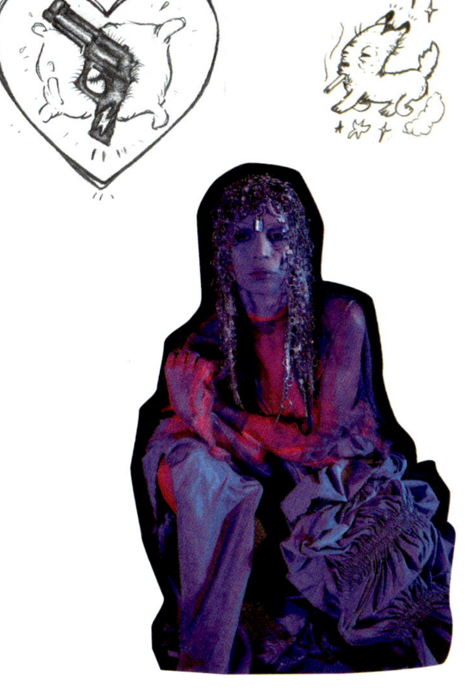
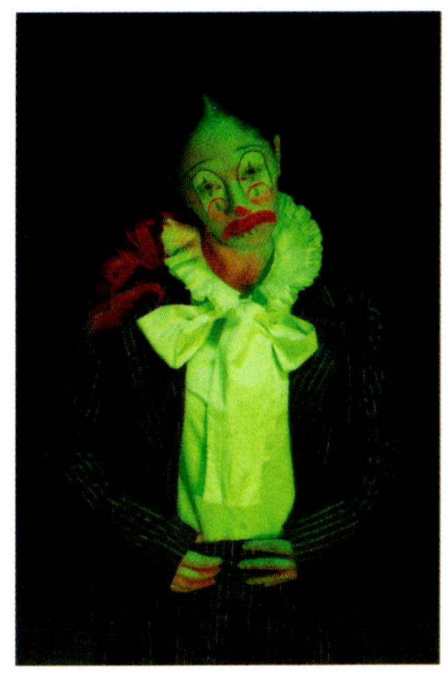
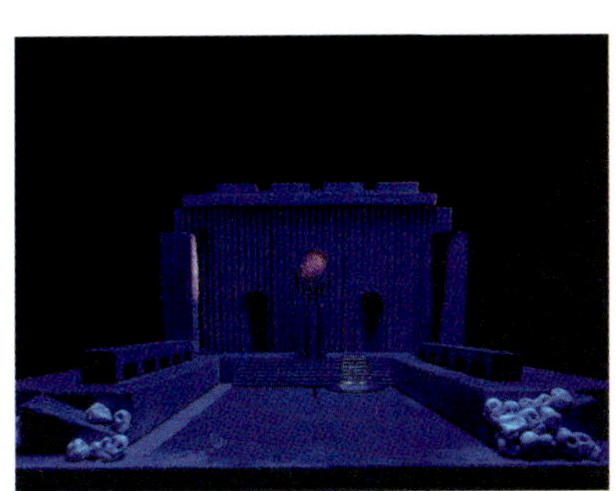
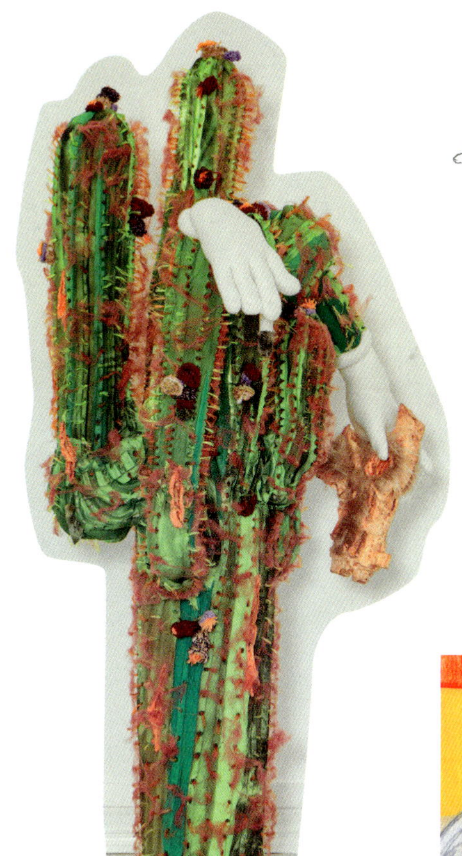
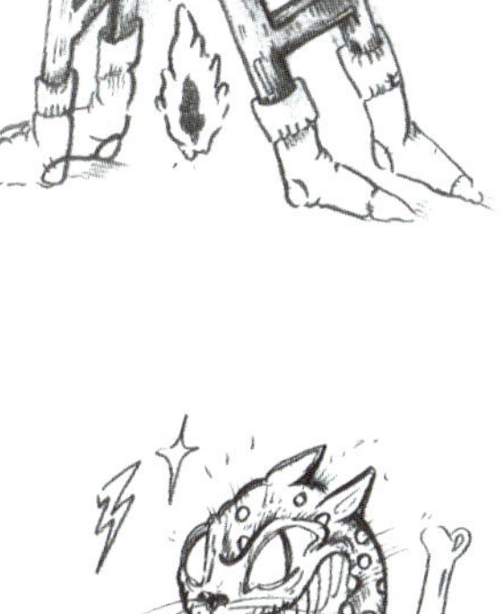
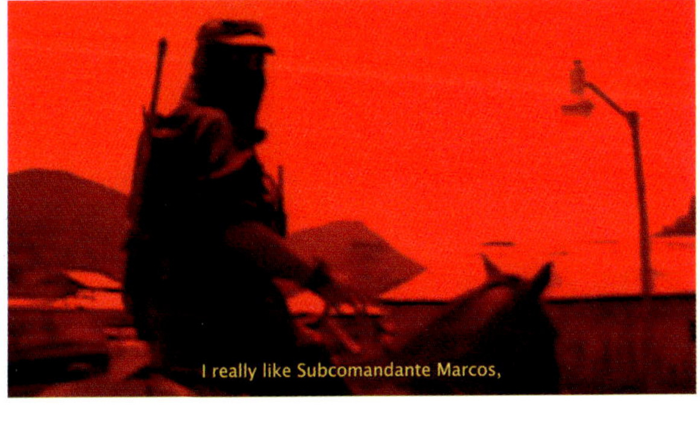
I really like Subcomandante Marcos,
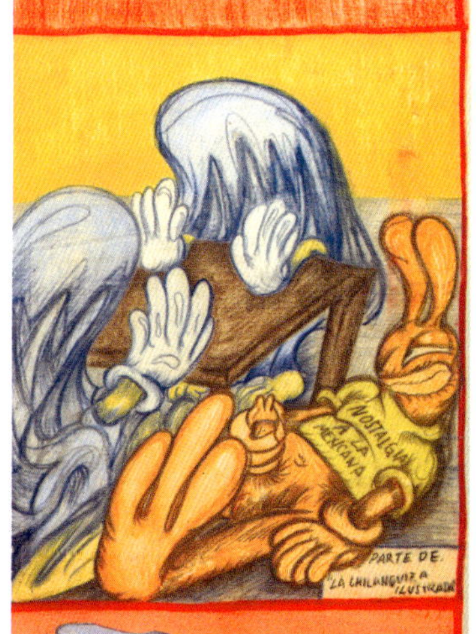
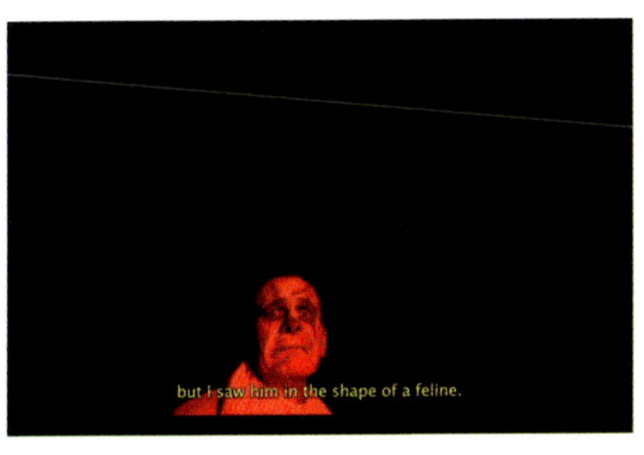
but I saw him in the shape of a feline.
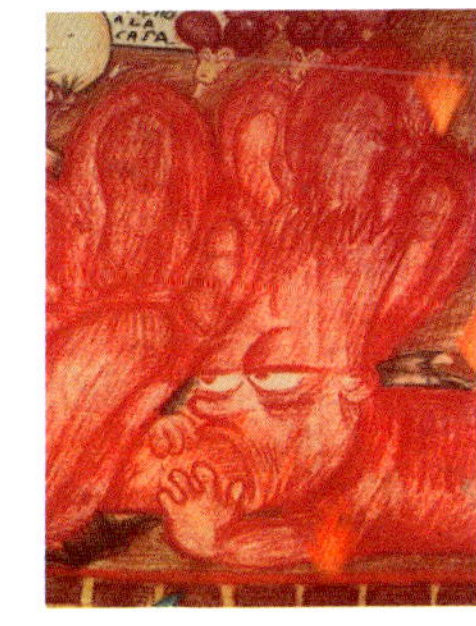
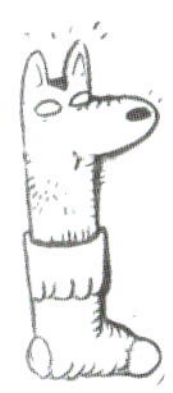

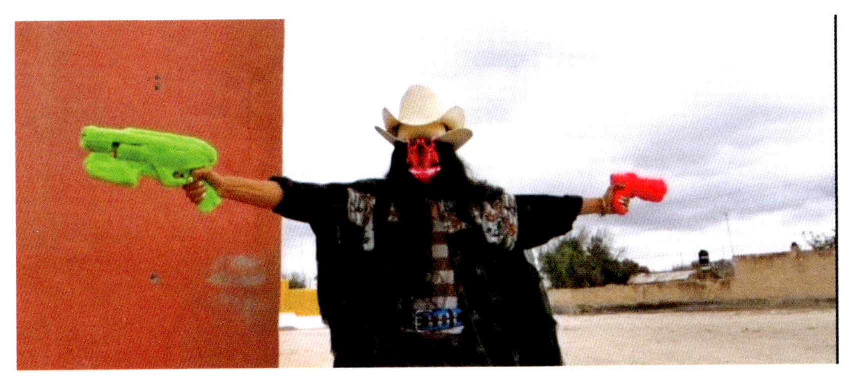

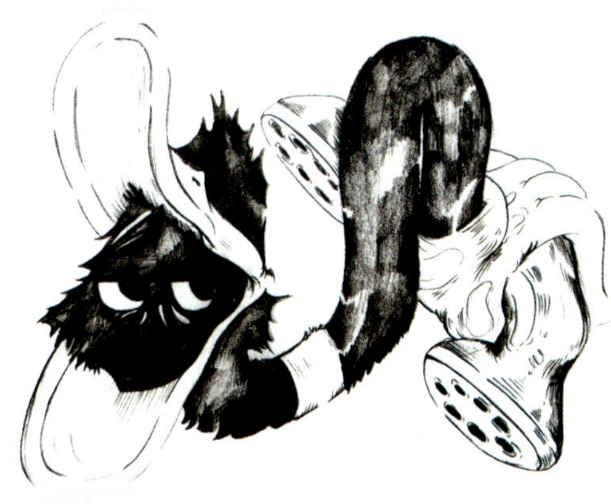

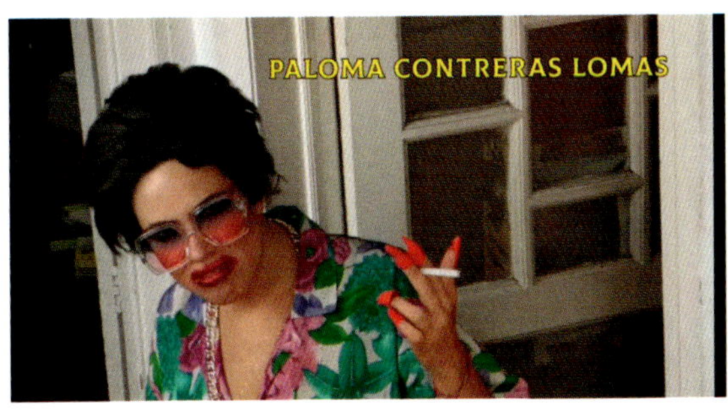
PALOMA CONTRERAS LOMAS

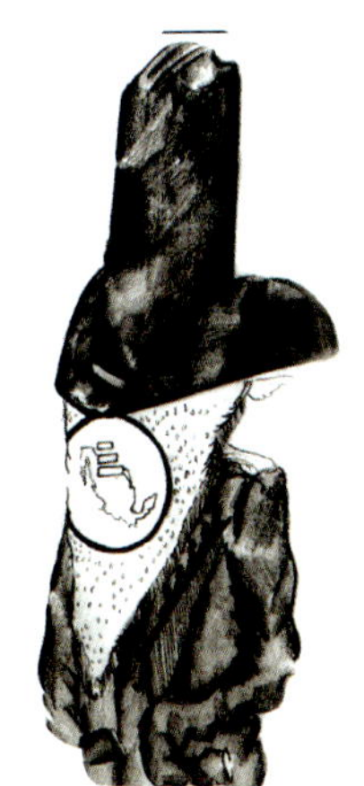

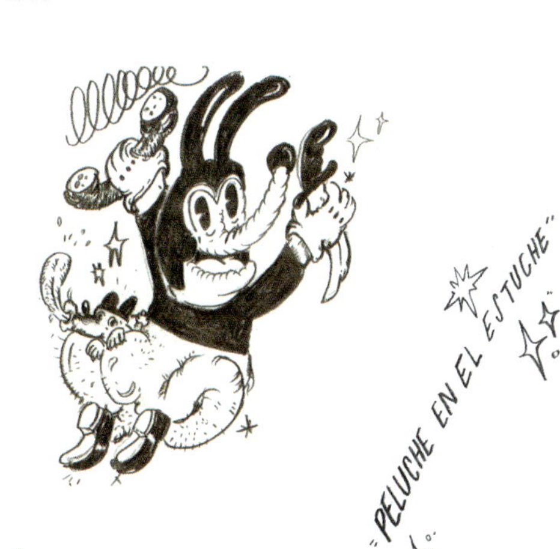
"PELUCHE EN EL ESTUCHE"

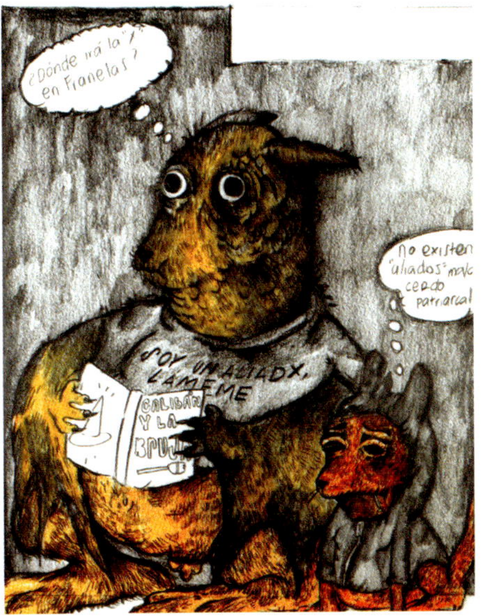
¿Dónde 'tá la
en Franela?
No existen
'aliados' malo
ce do
patriarcal
SOY UN ALIADX,
LAMEME
CALIBAN
Y LA
BRUJ

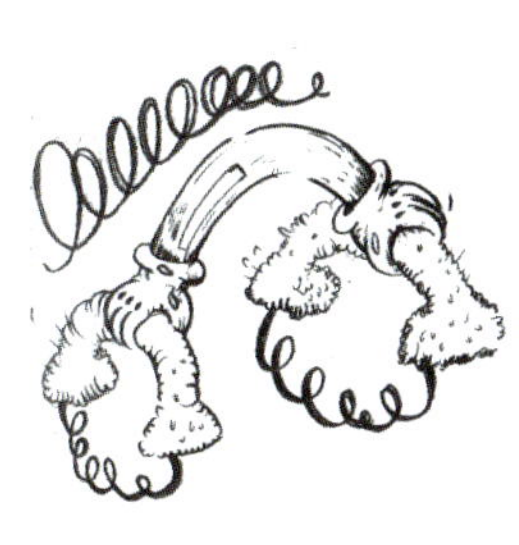

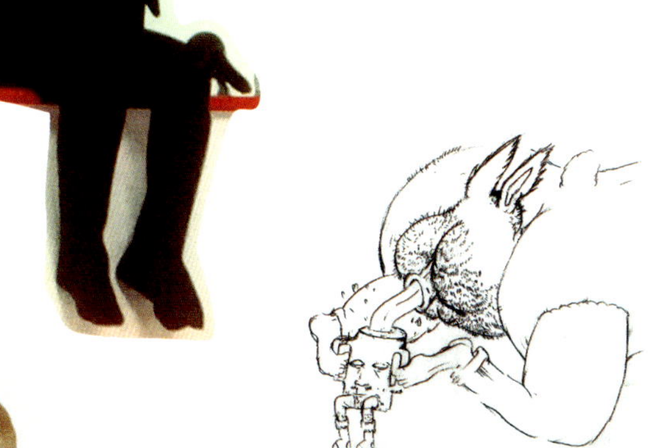
¡SÁBADO, DISTRITO FEDERAL!

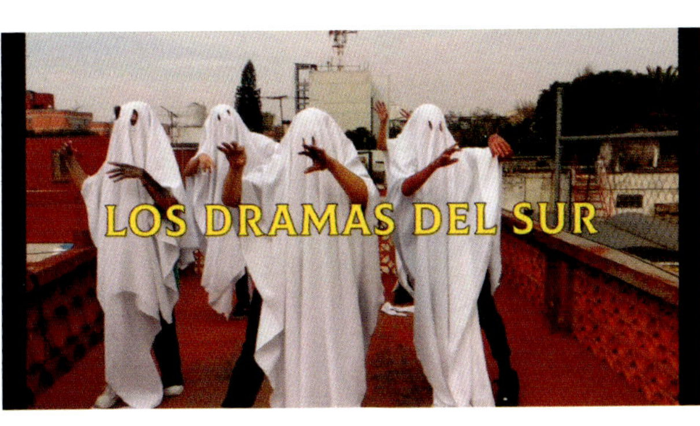
LOS DRAMAS DEL SUR

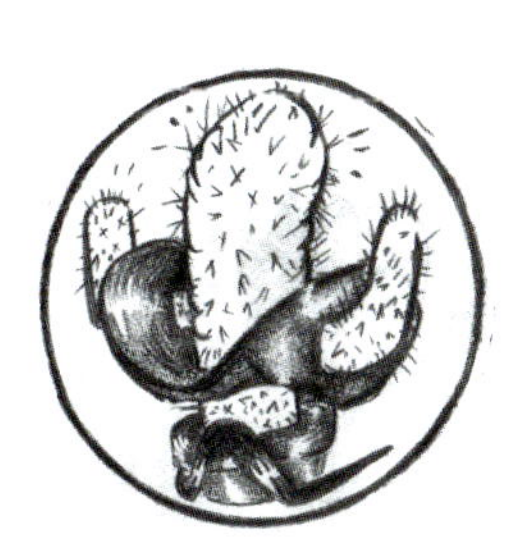

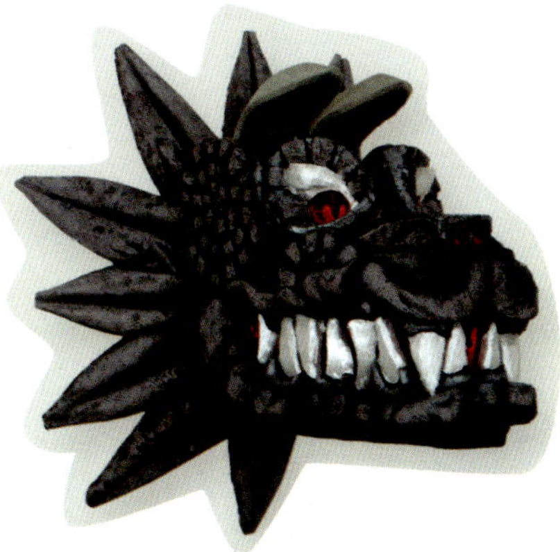

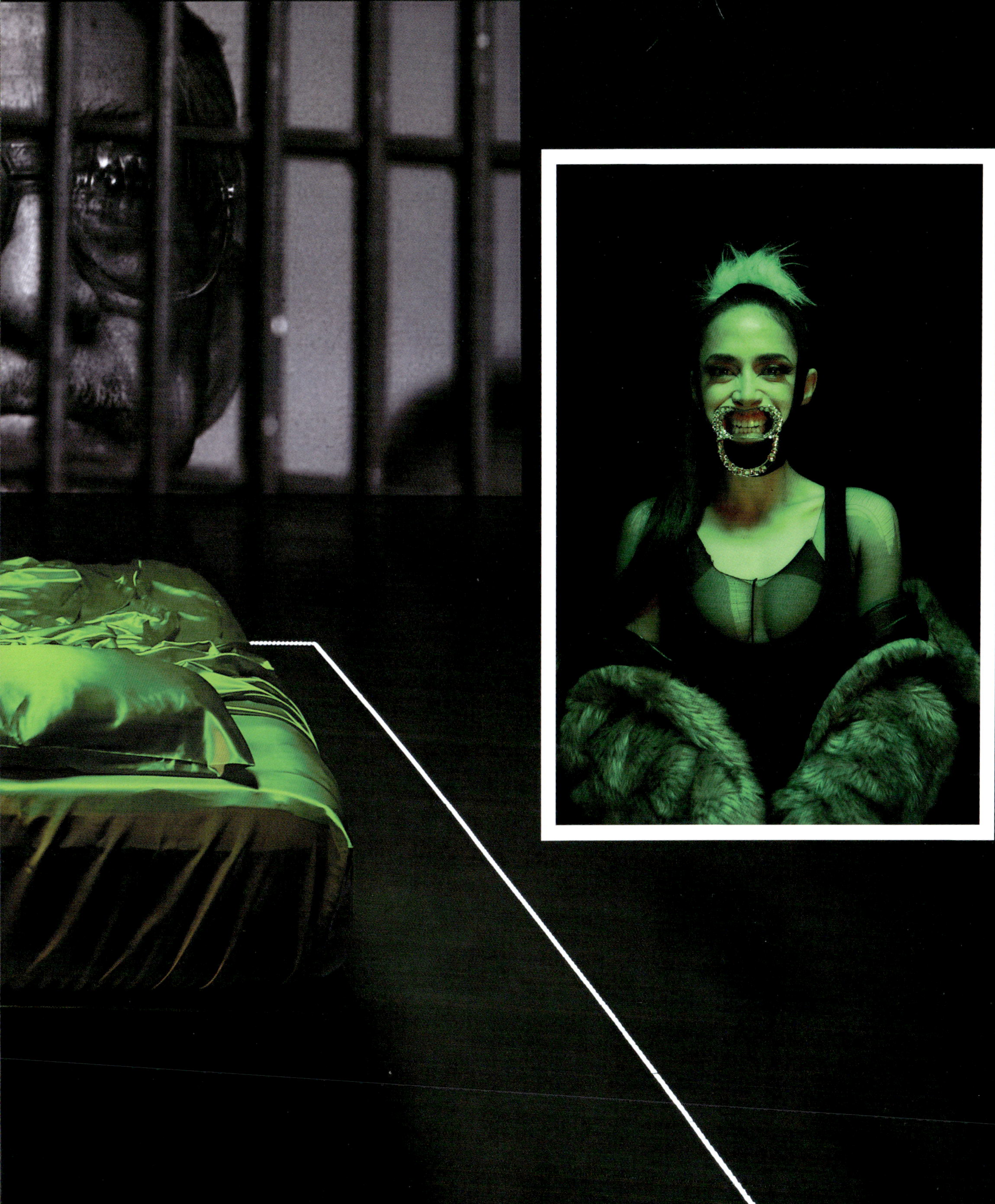

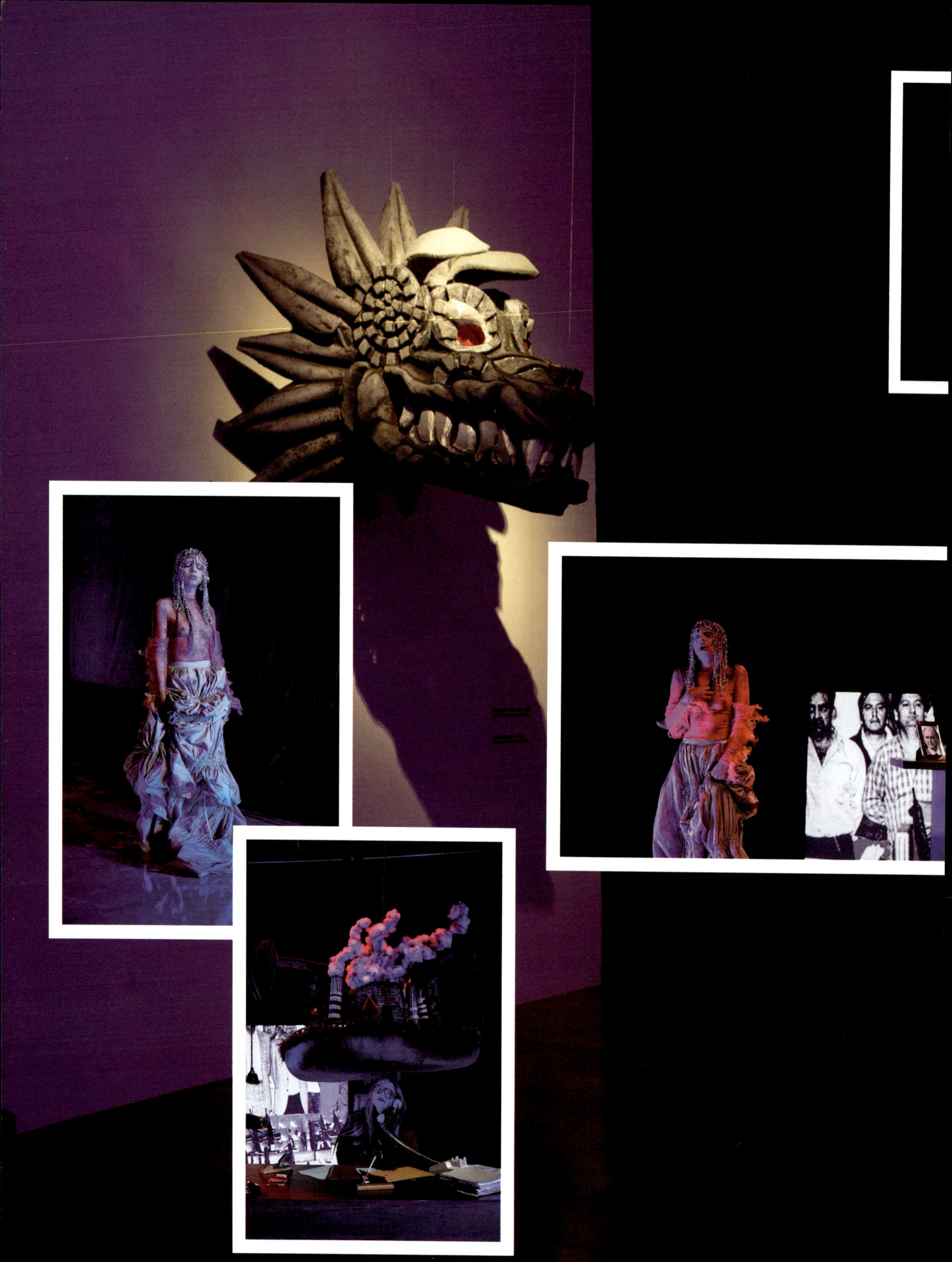

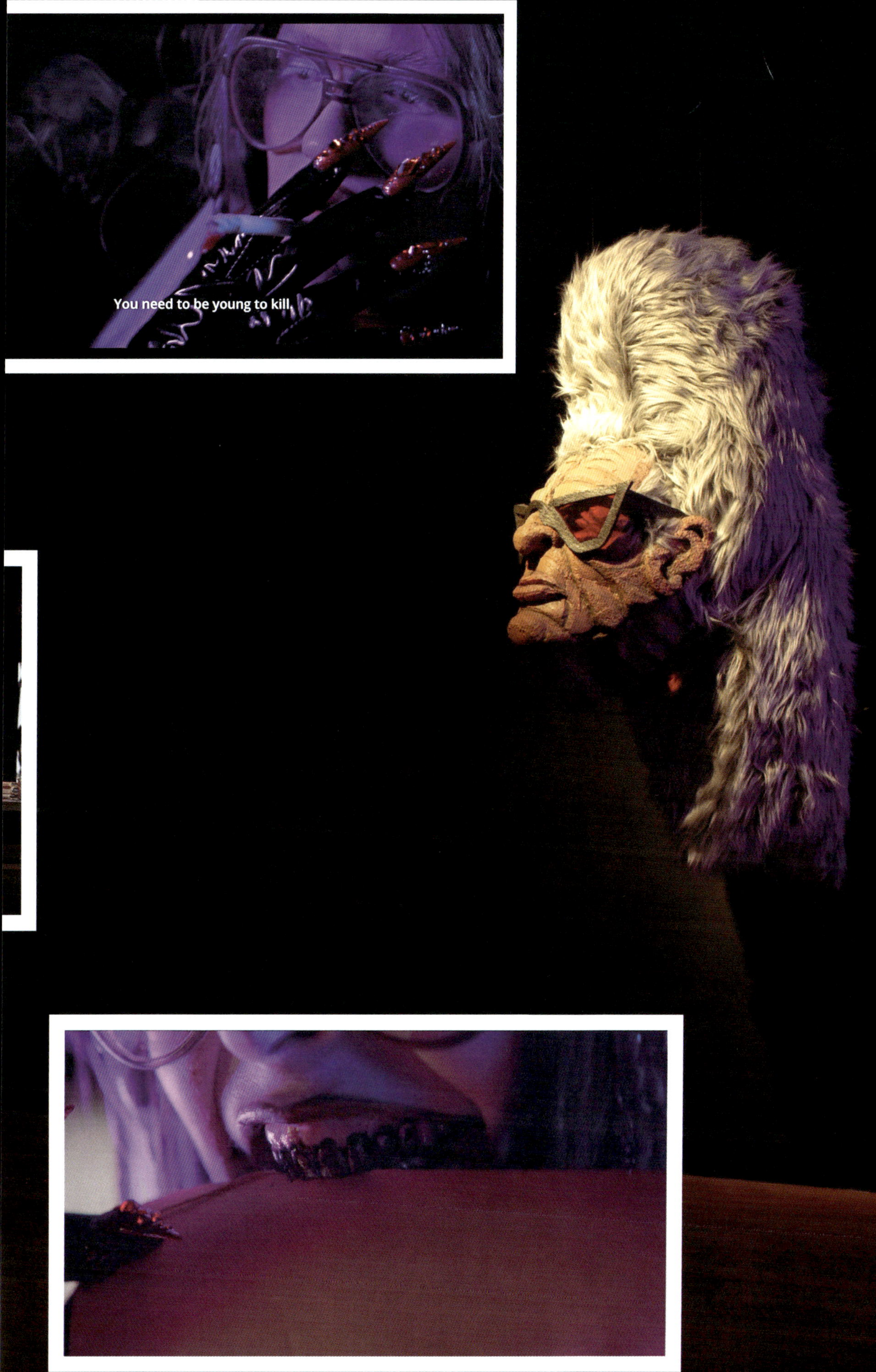
You need to be young to kill.

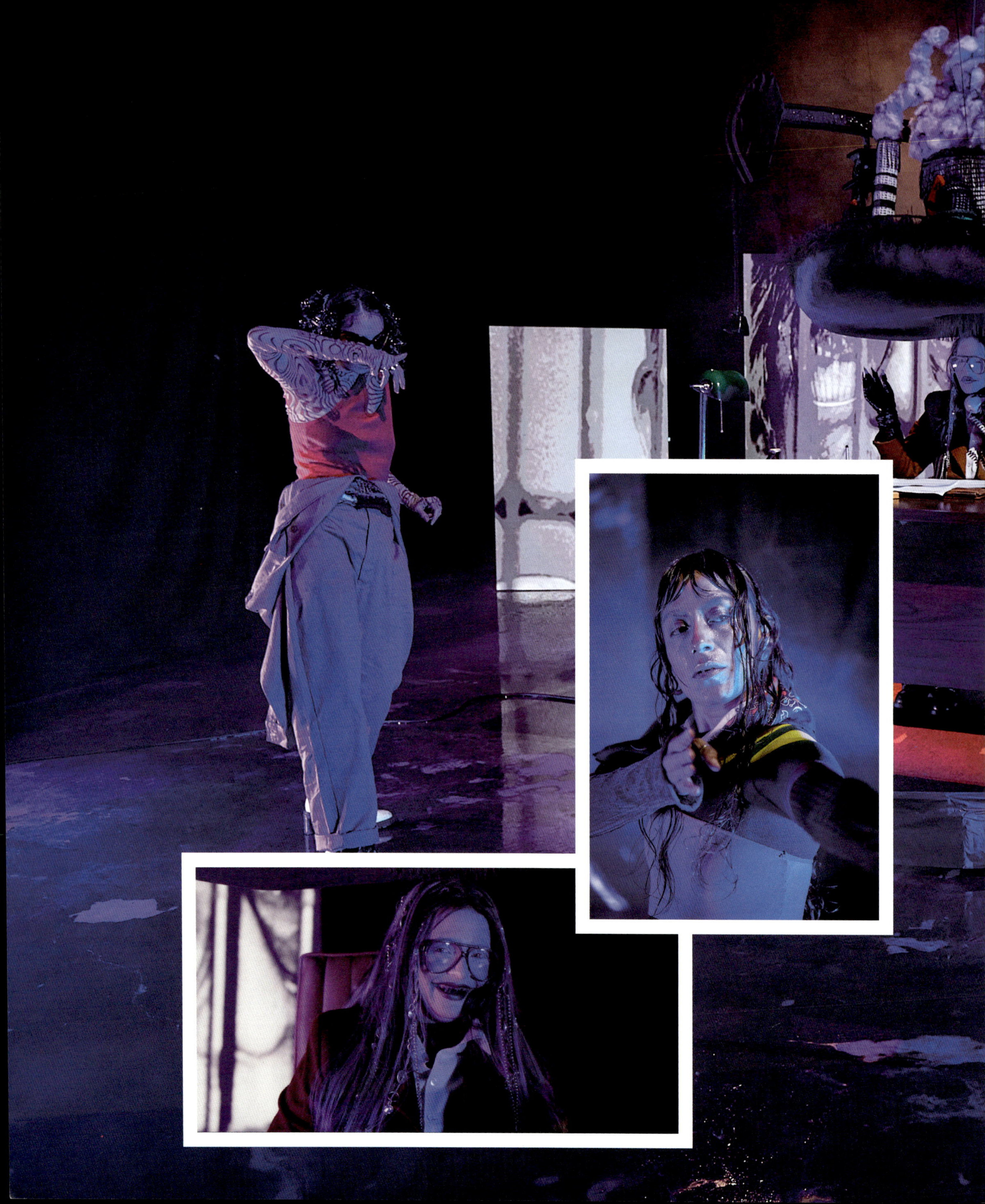

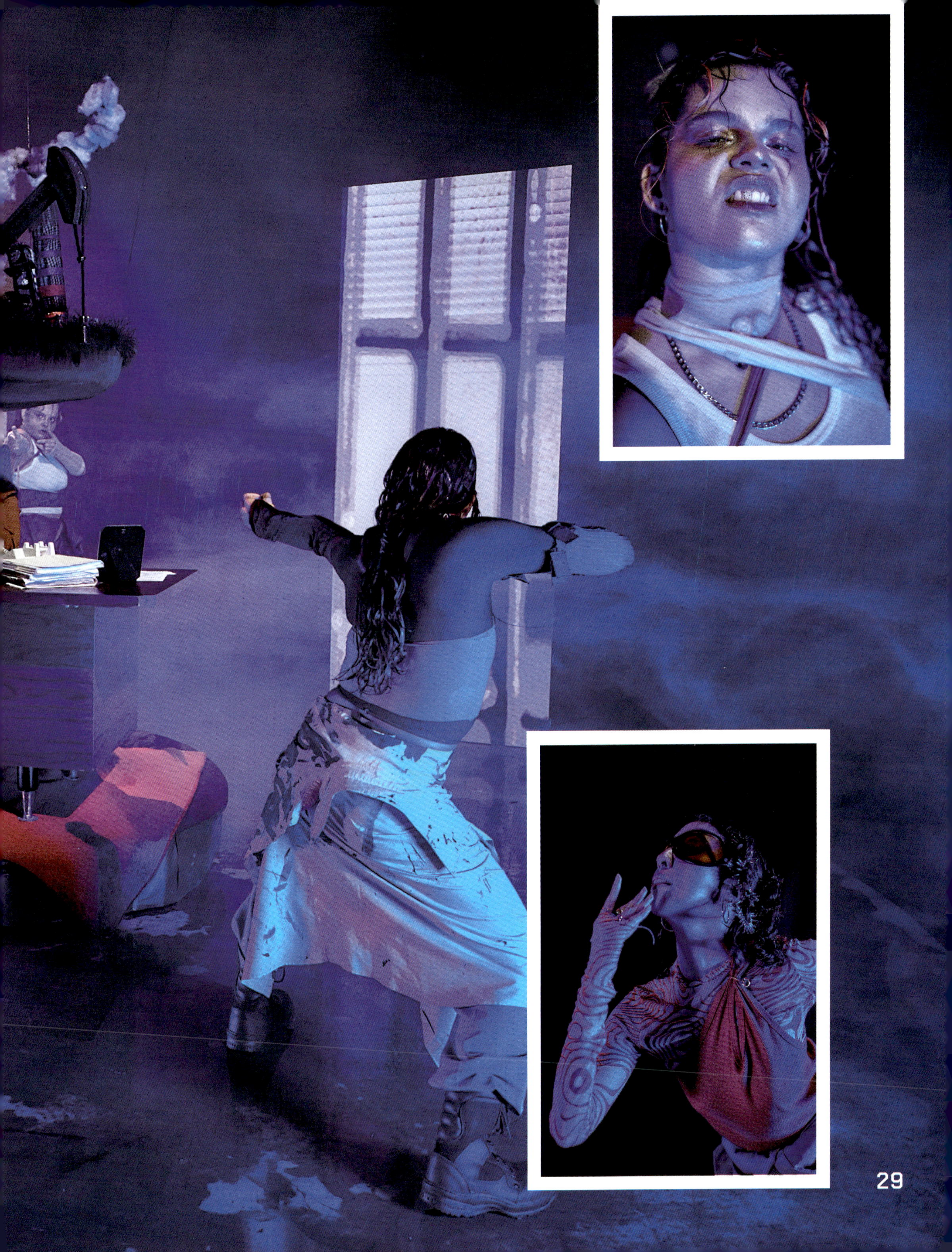

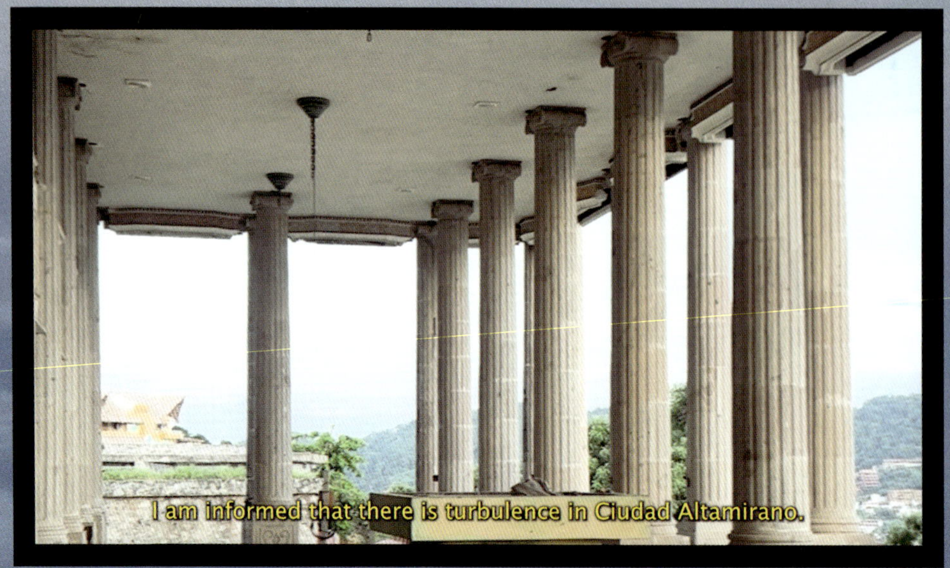

I am informed that there is turbulence in Ciudad Altamirano.

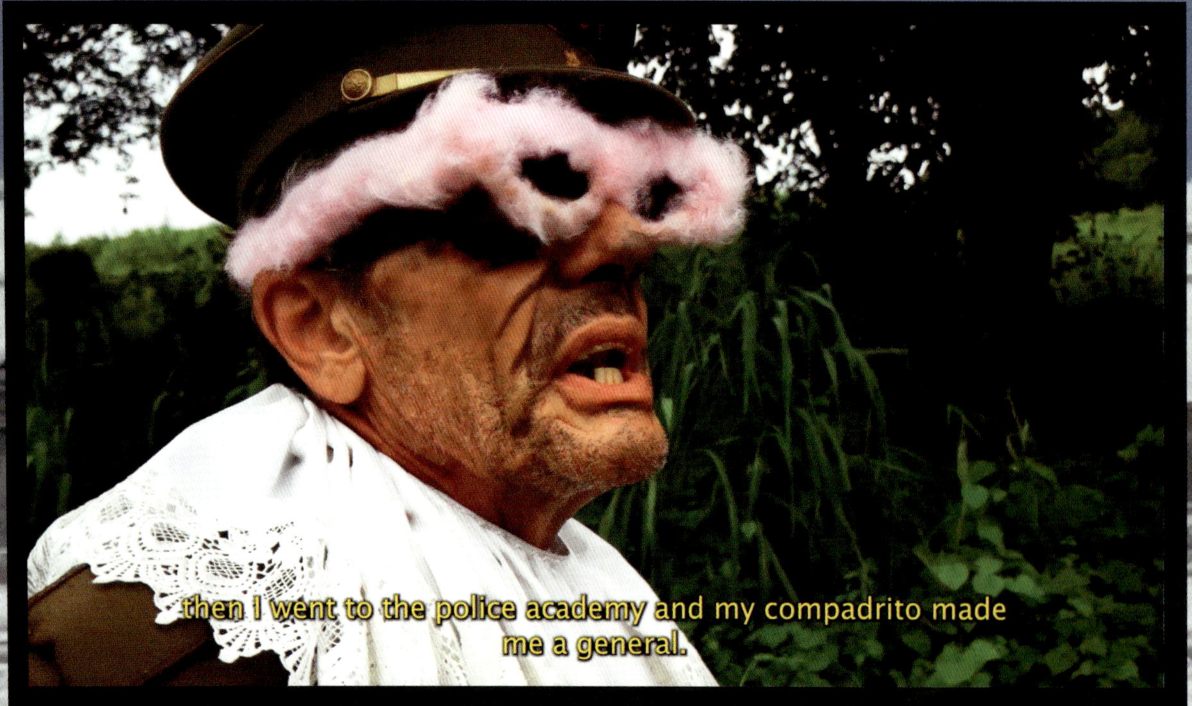

then I went to the police academy and my compadrito made
me a general.

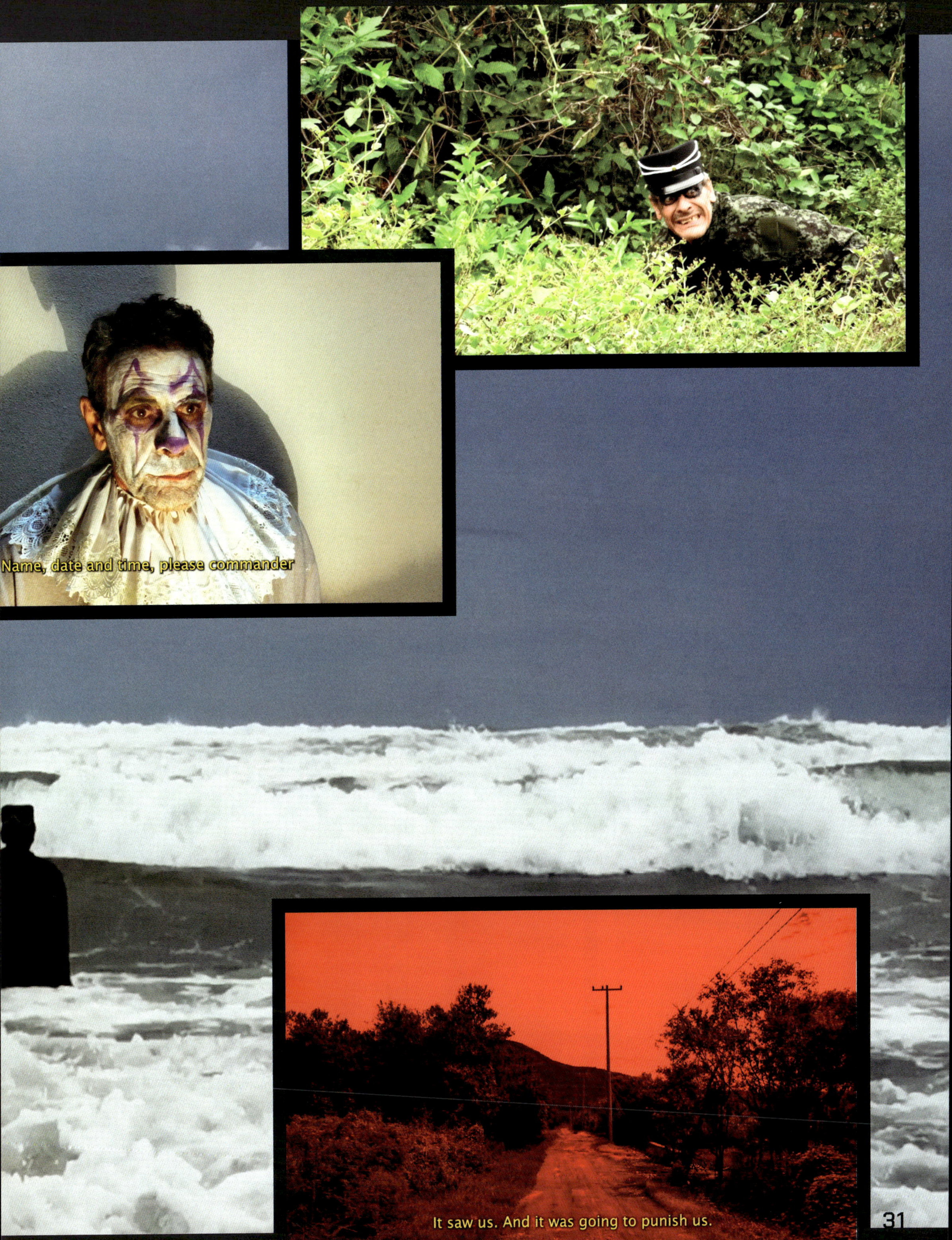
Name, date and time, please commander
It saw us. And it was going to punish us.

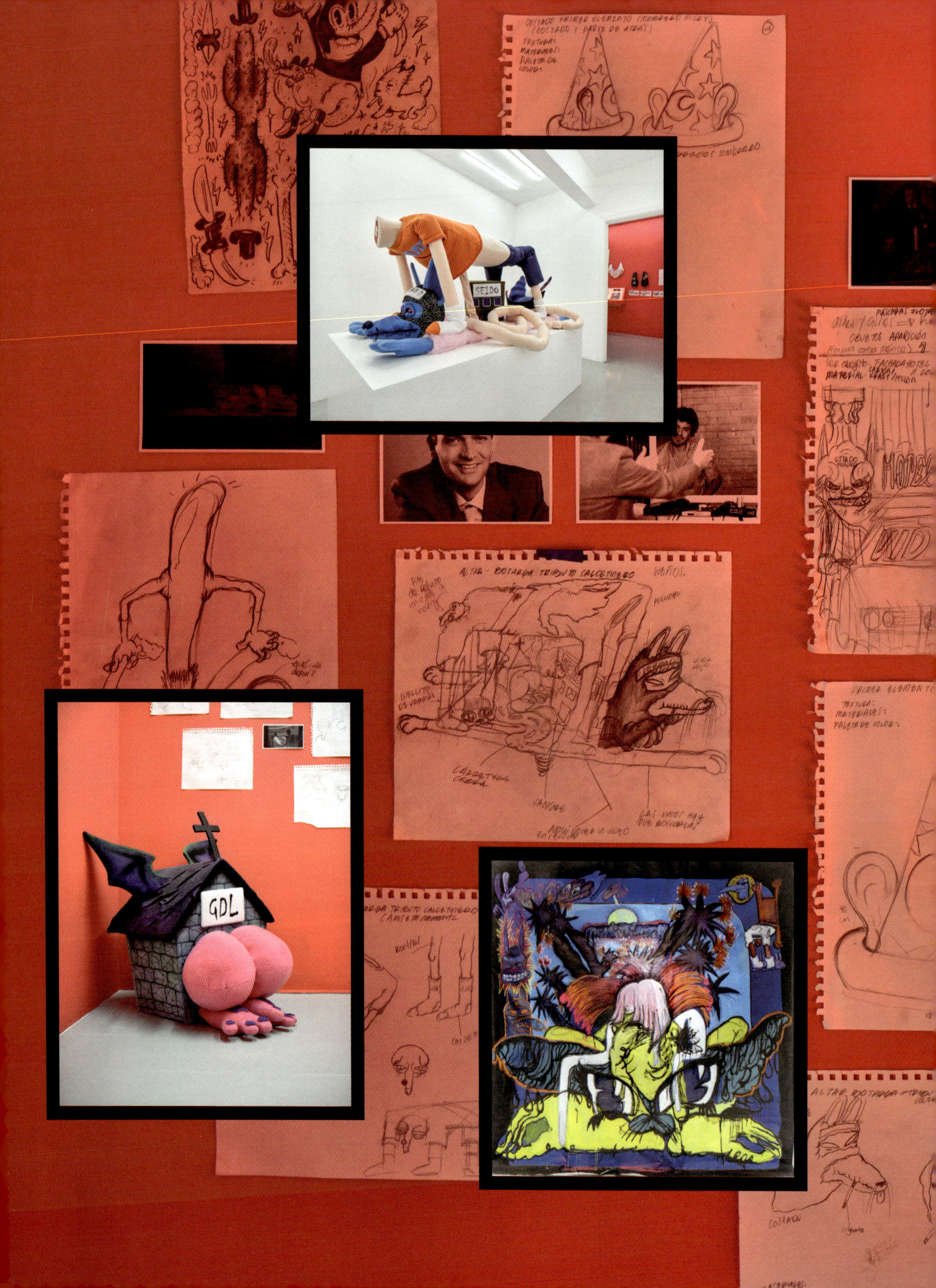
SEIDO
GDL

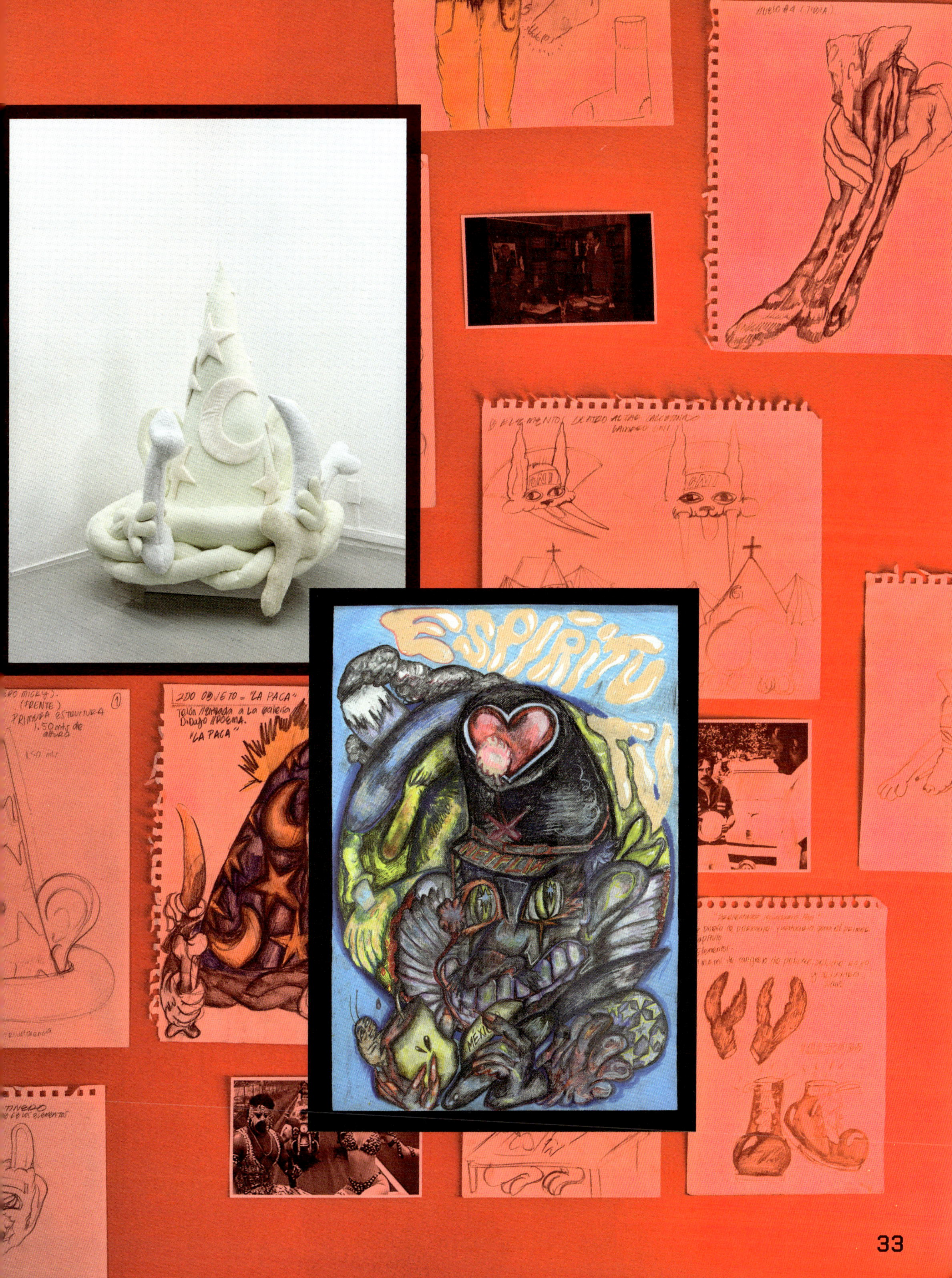

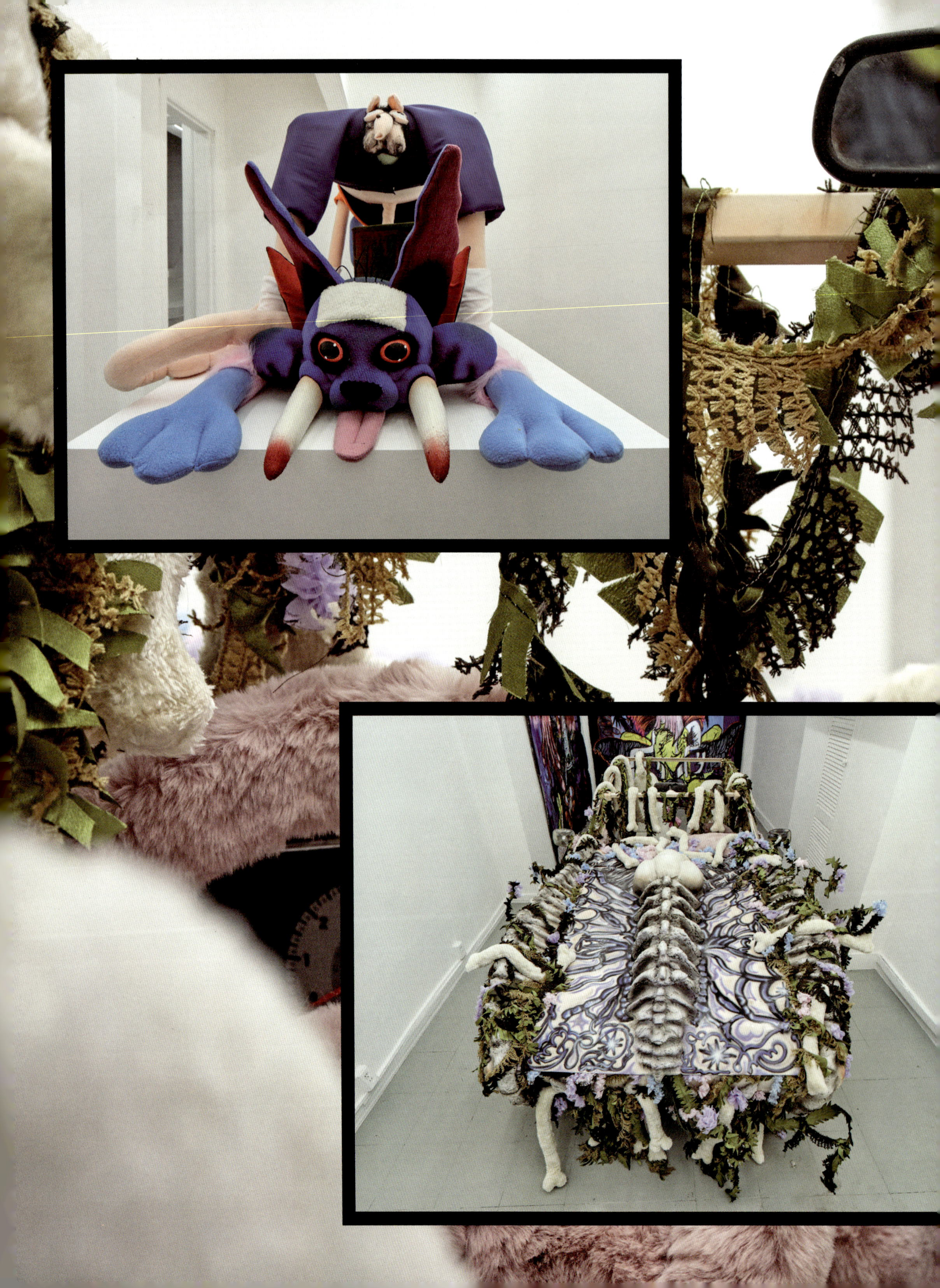

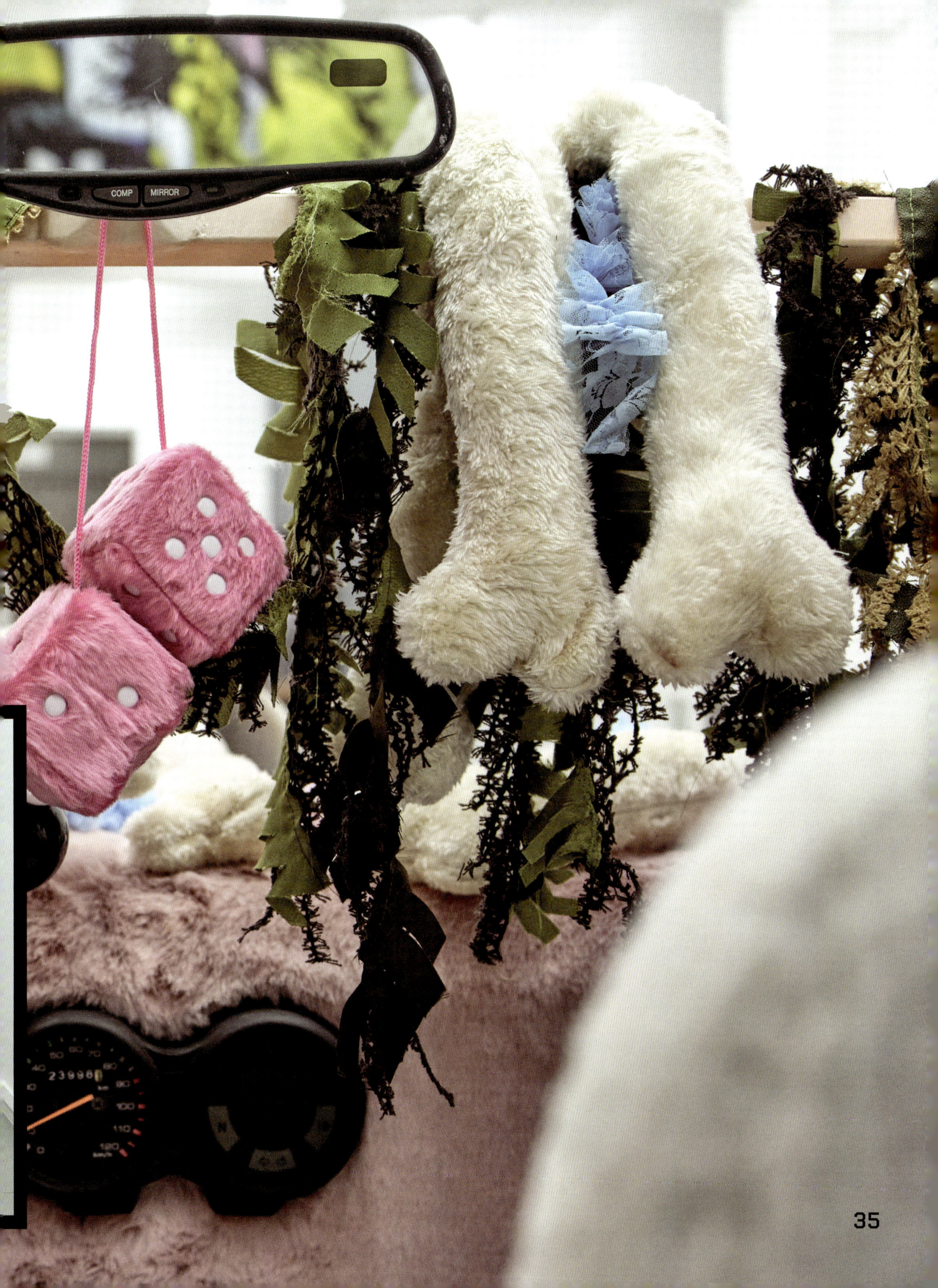

COMP
MIRROR

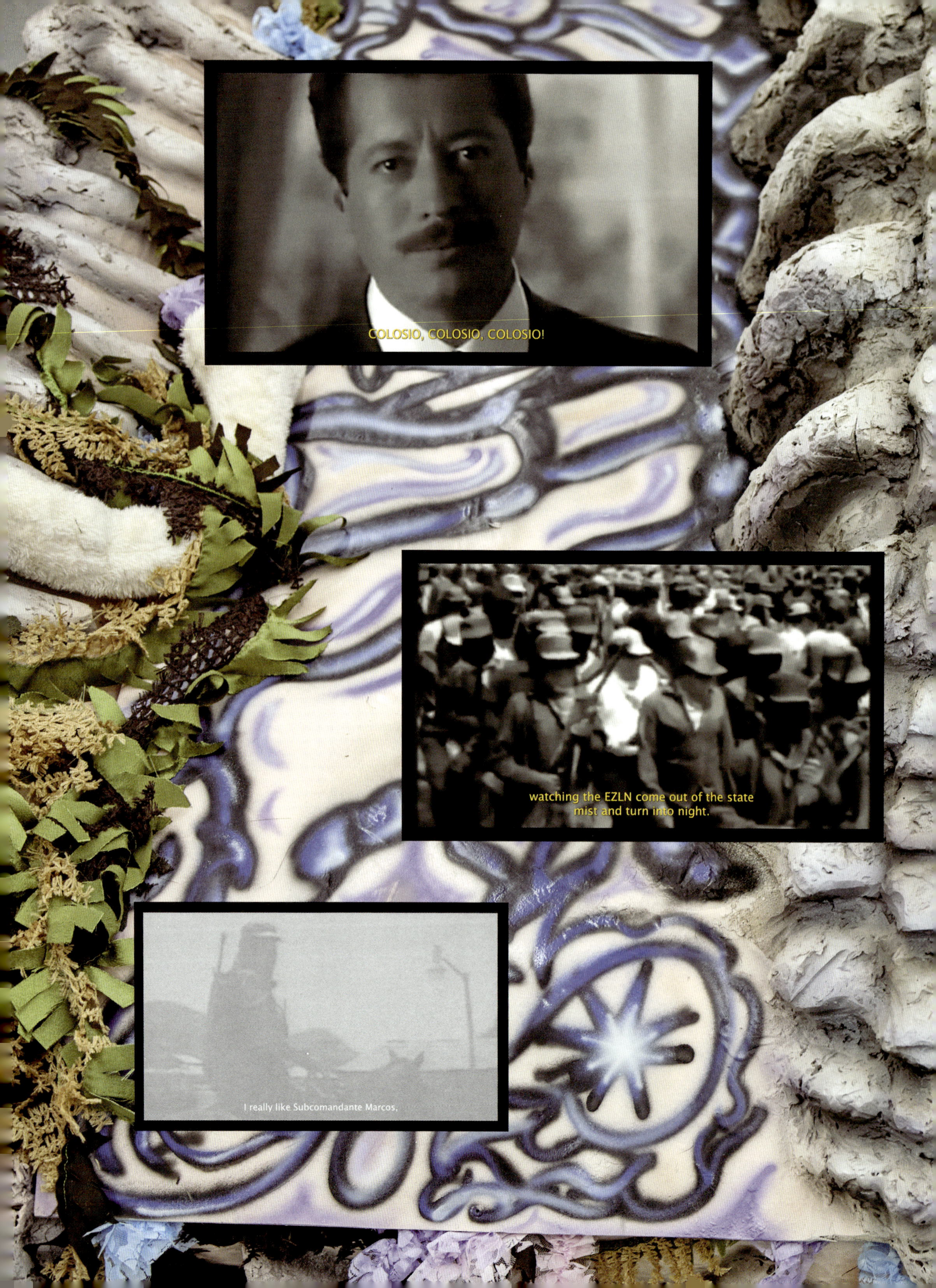
COLOSIO, COLOSIO, COLOSIO!
watching the EZLN come out of the state
mist and turn into night.
I really like Subcomandante Marcos,

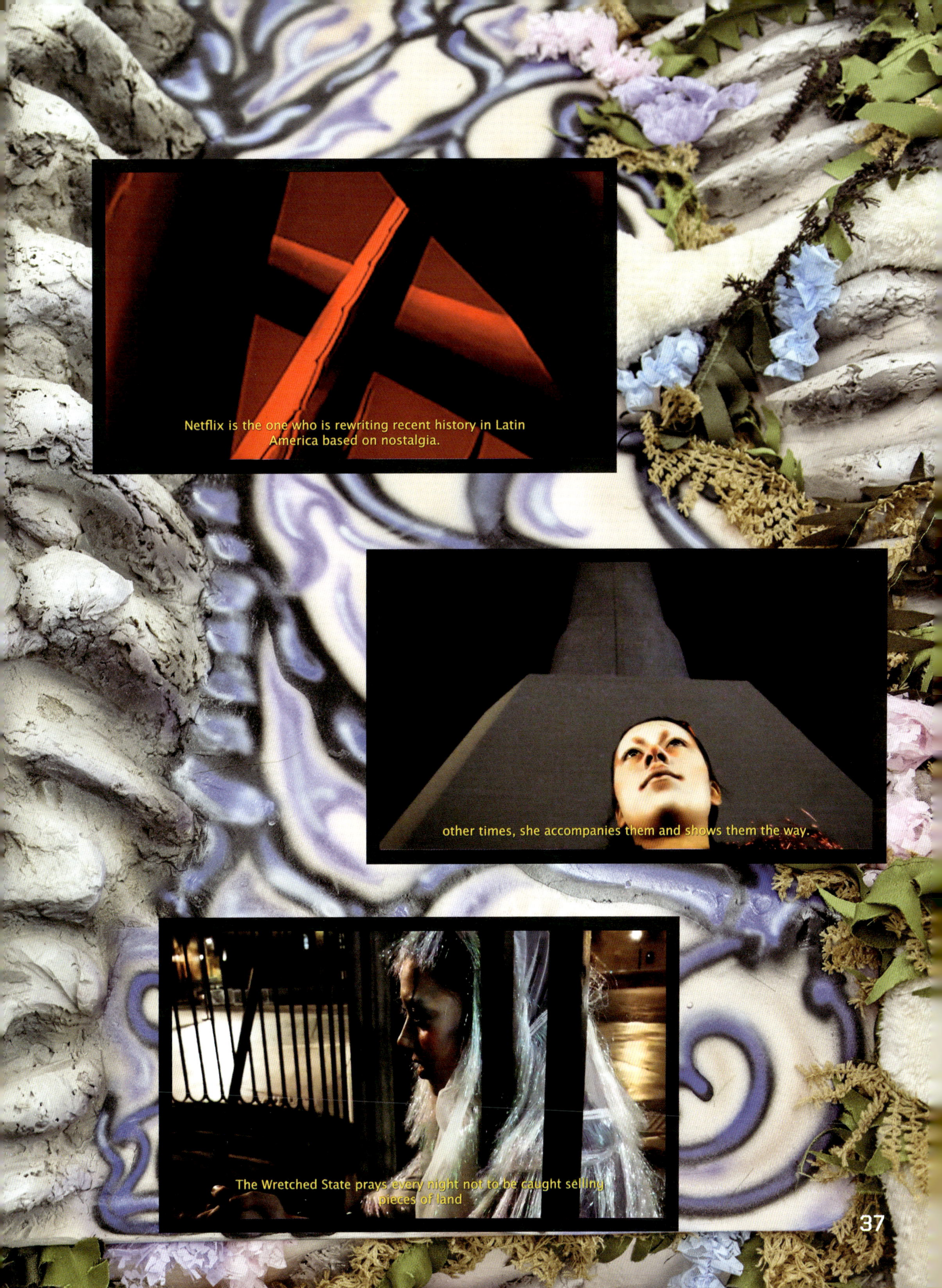

Netflix is the one who is rewriting recent history in Latin America based on nostalgia.

other times, she accompanies them and shows them the way.

The Wretched State prays every night not to be caught selling pieces of land

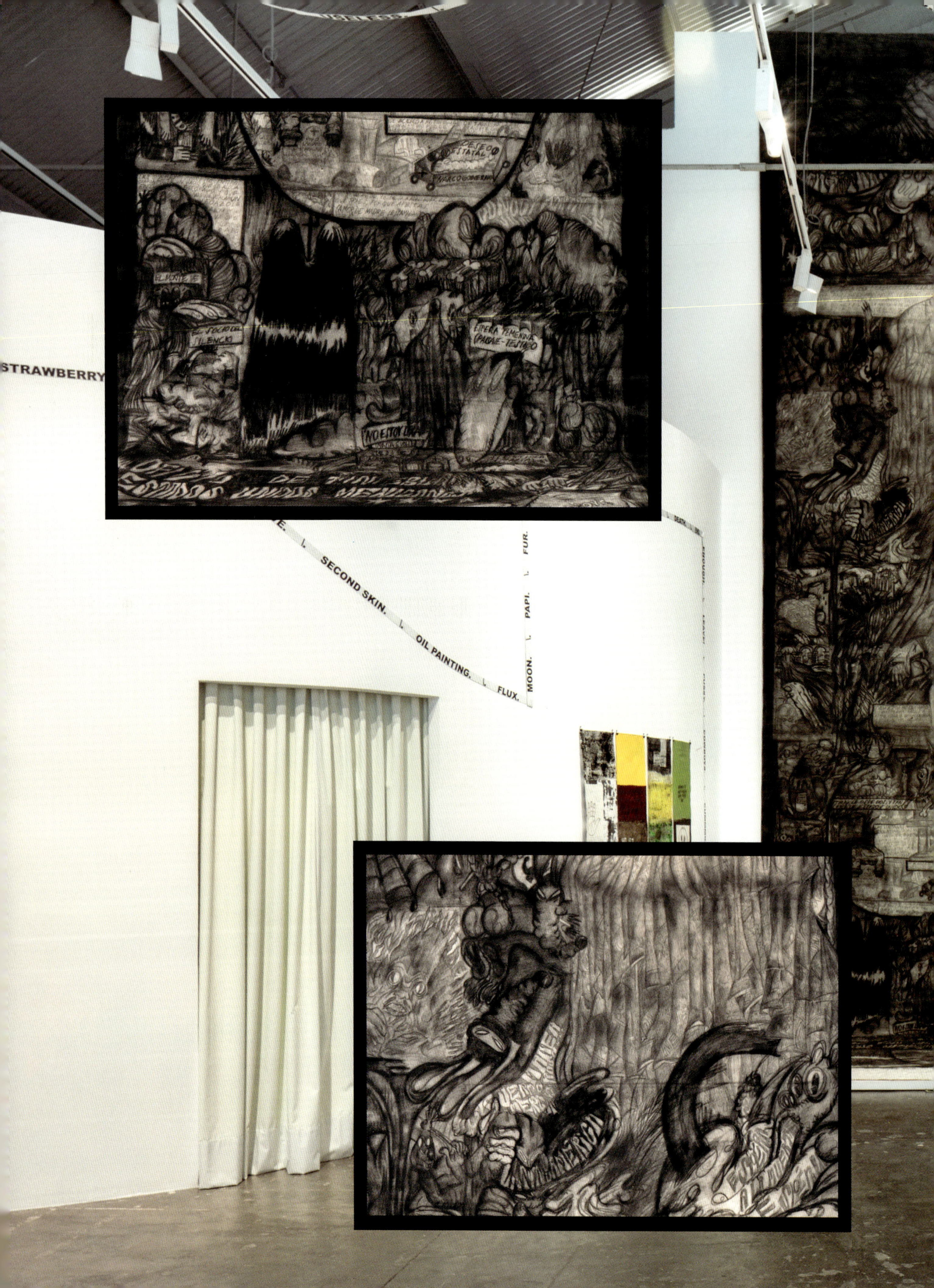
STRAWBERRY
SECOND SKIN.
OIL PAINTING.
FLUX.
MOON.
PAPI.
FUR.
DEATH

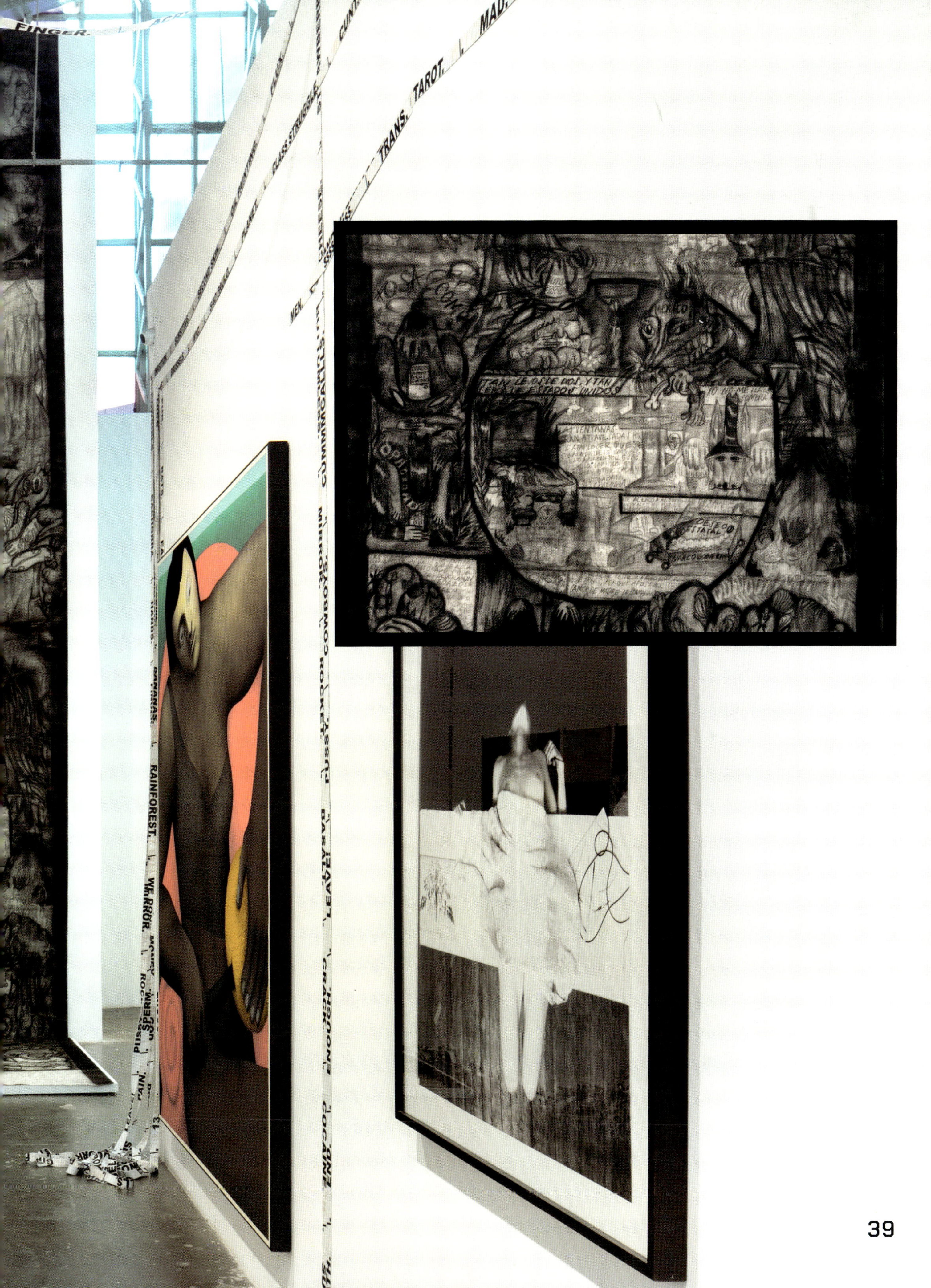

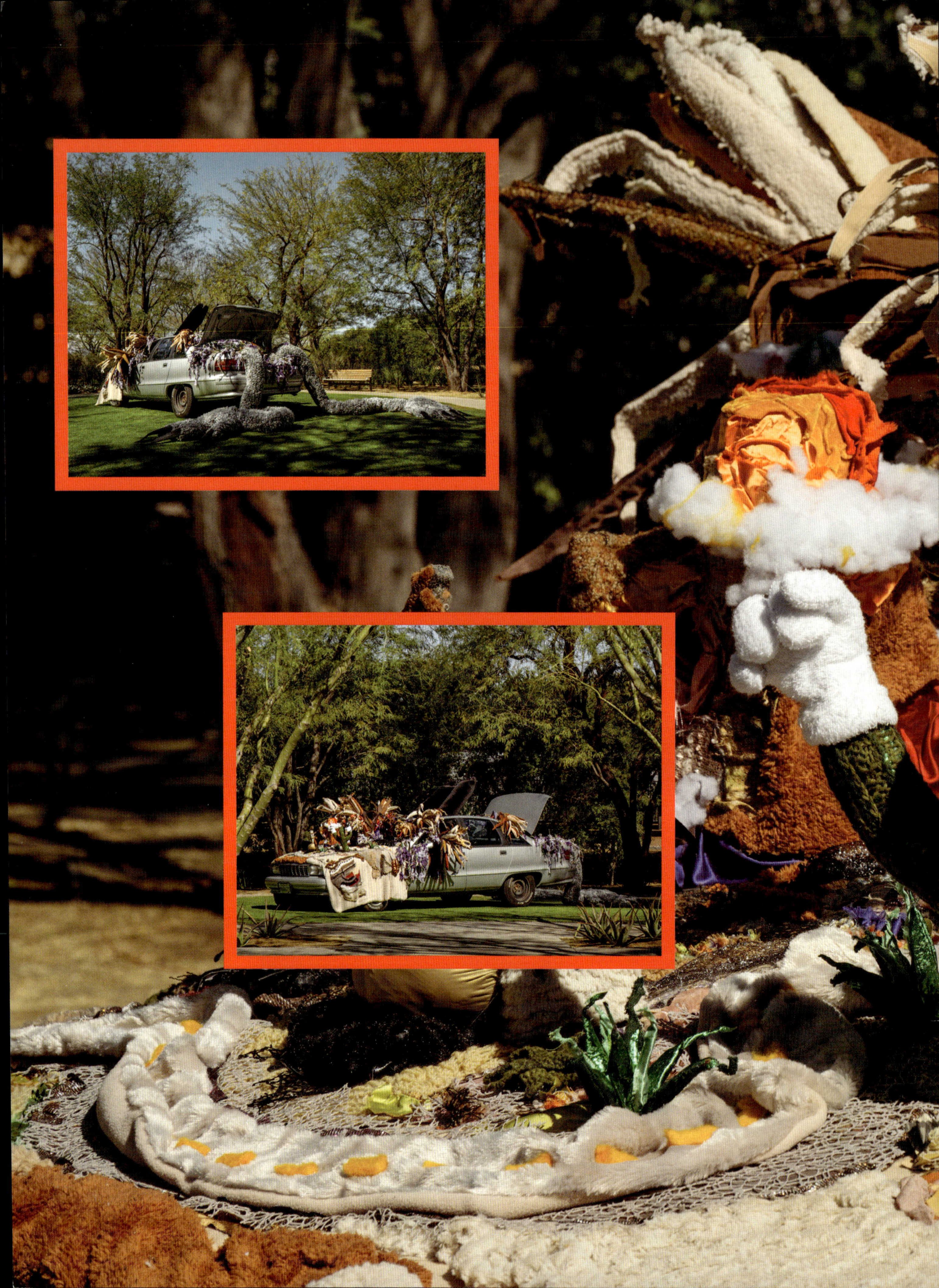

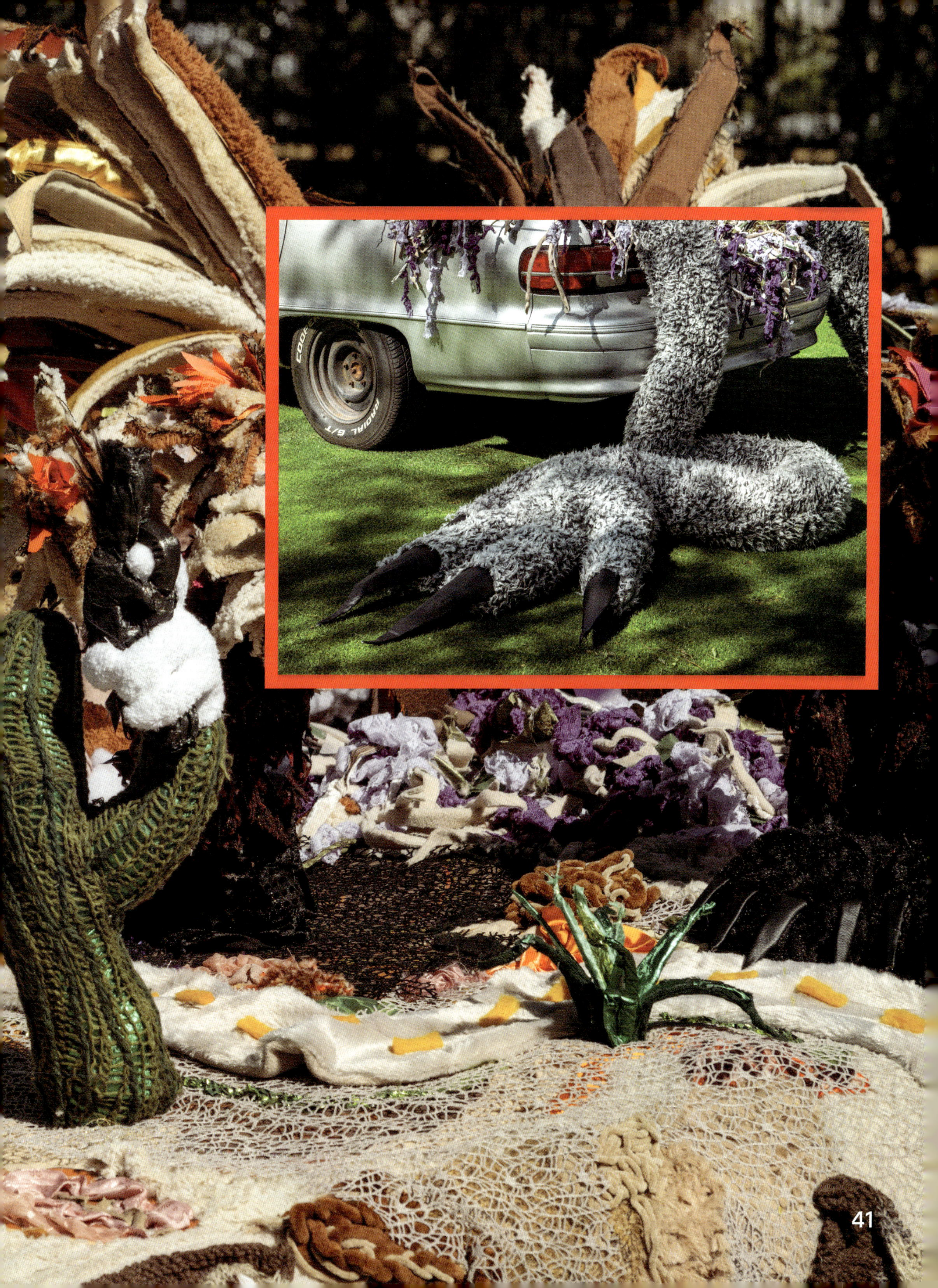

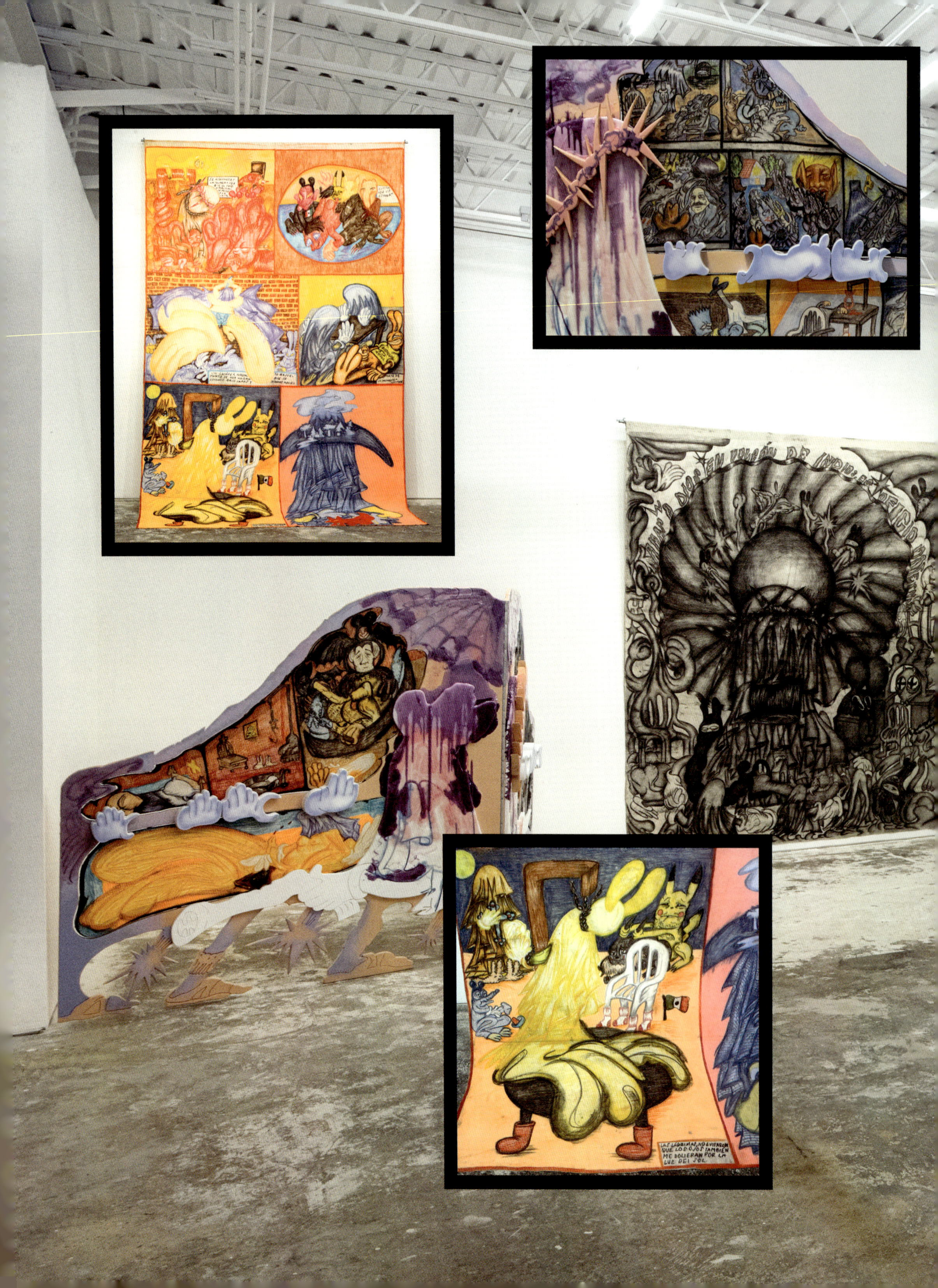

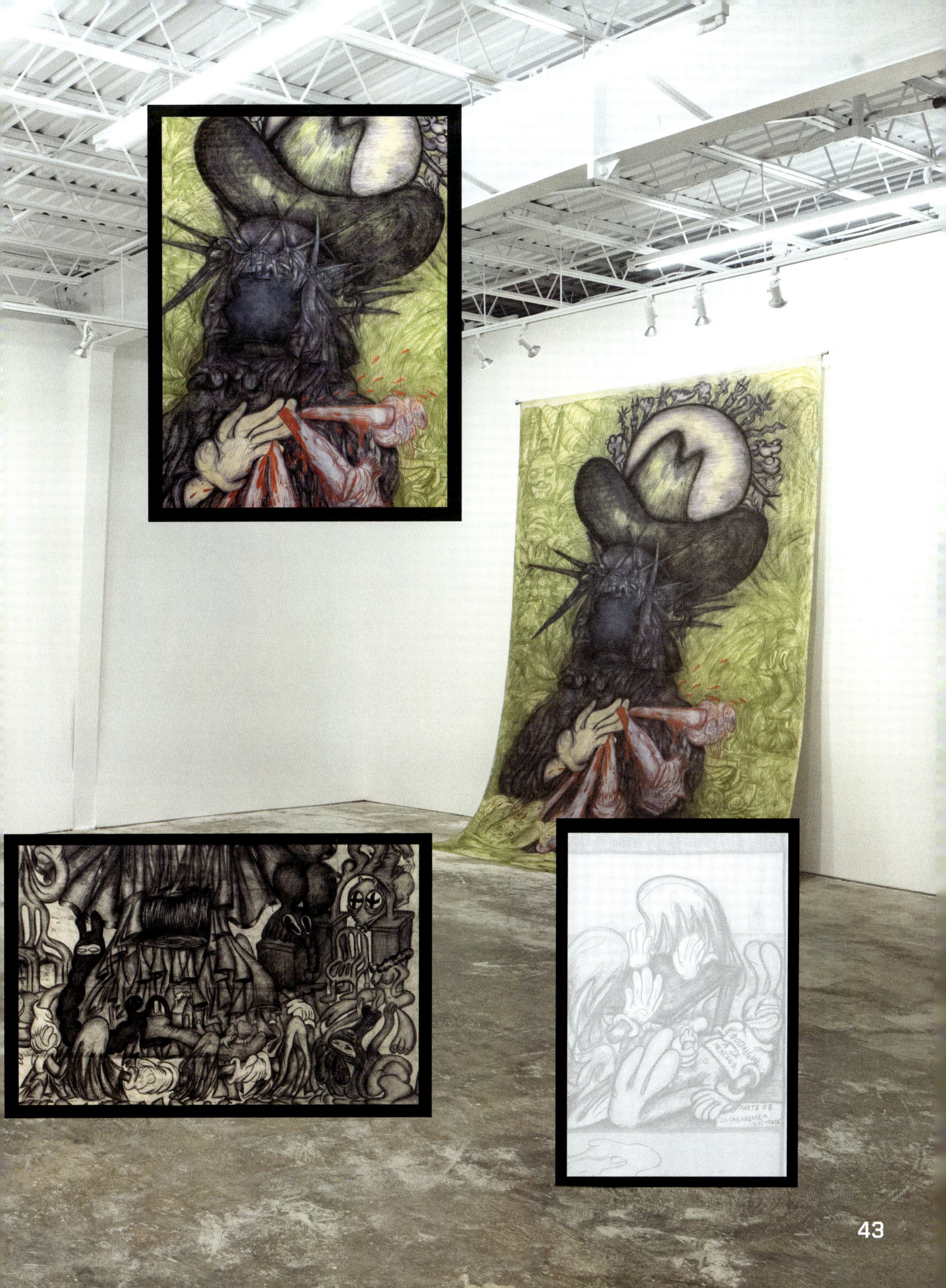

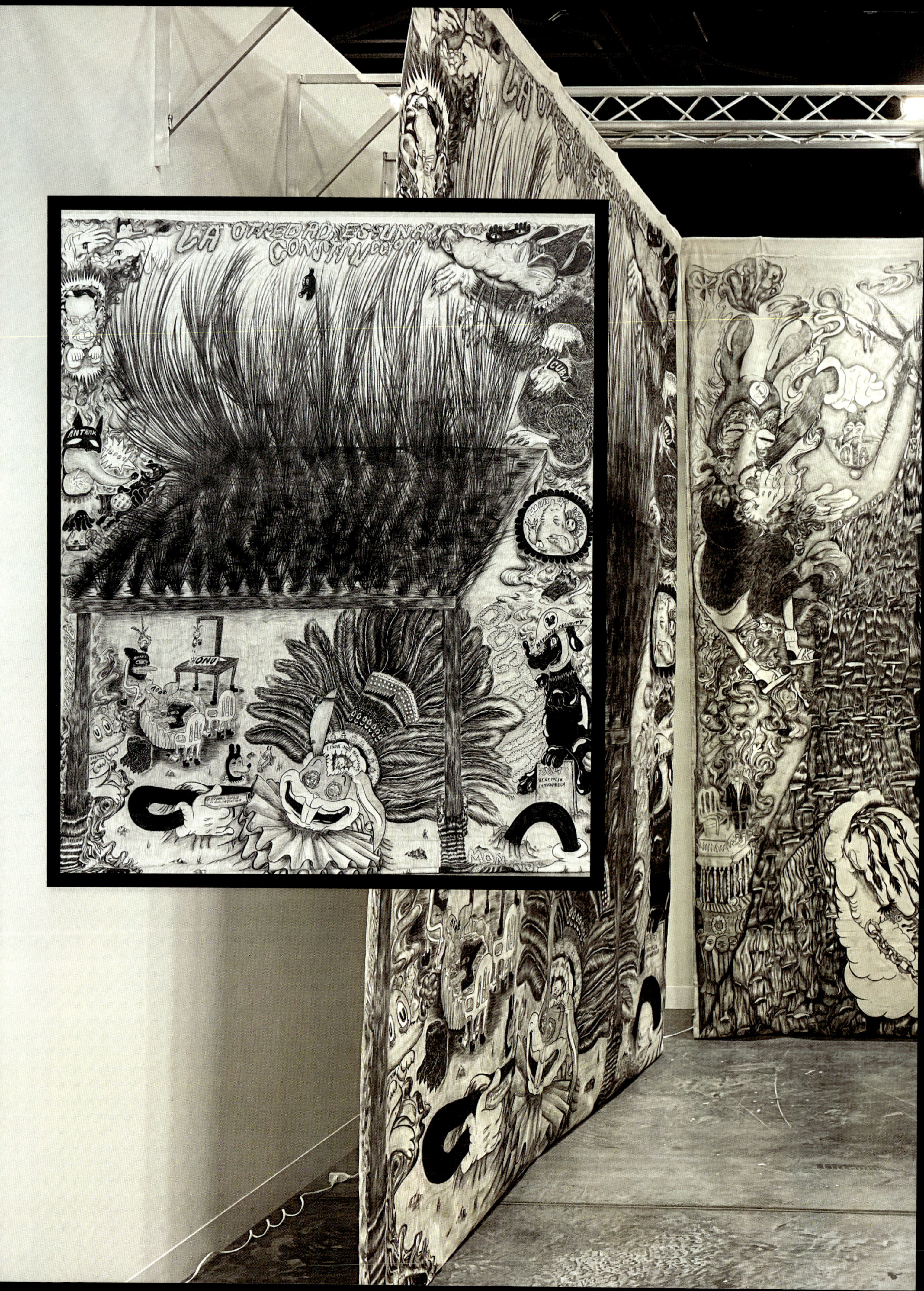

LA OTREDAD ES UNA
CONSTRUCCION
ONU
CUBA

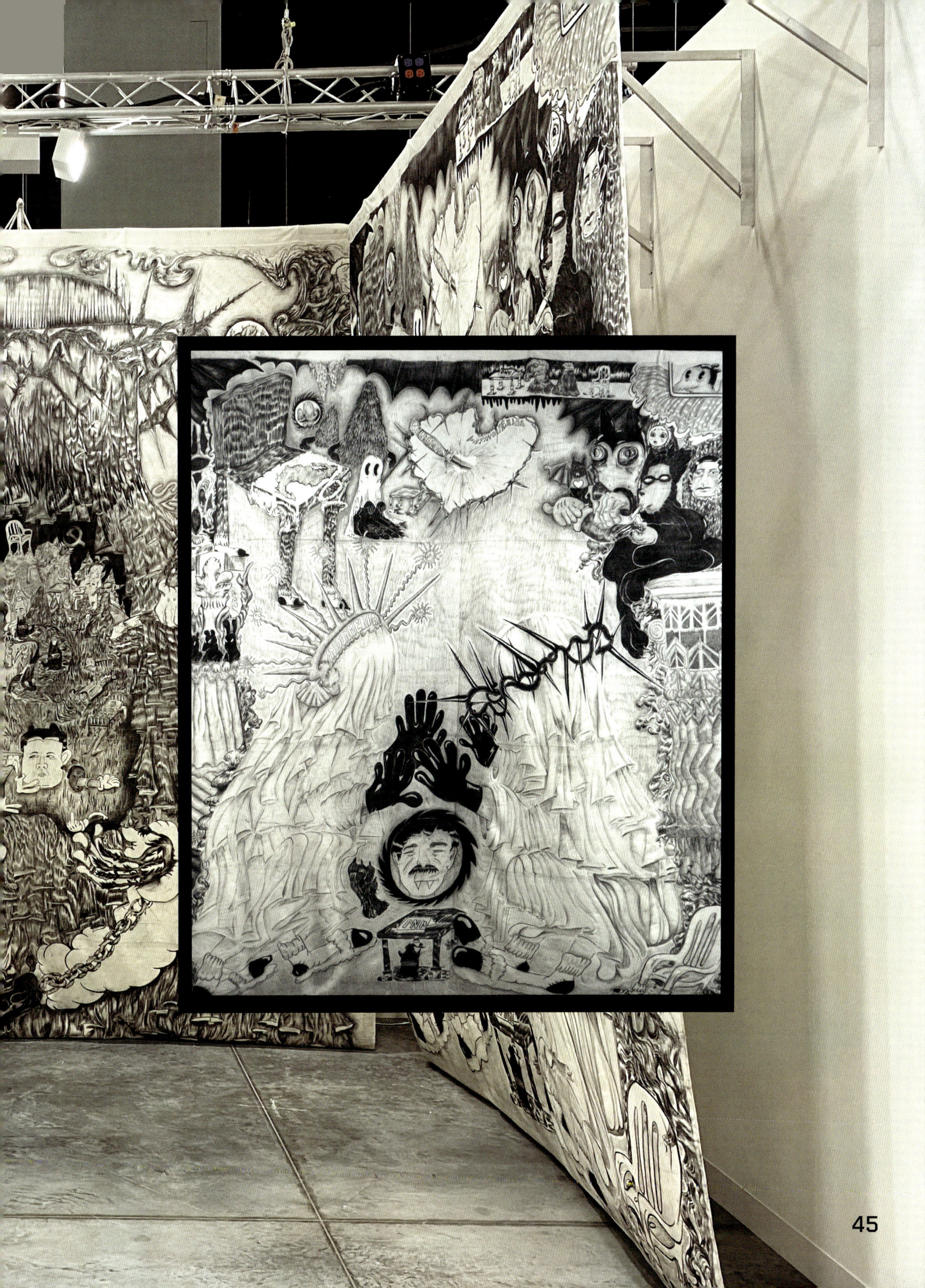

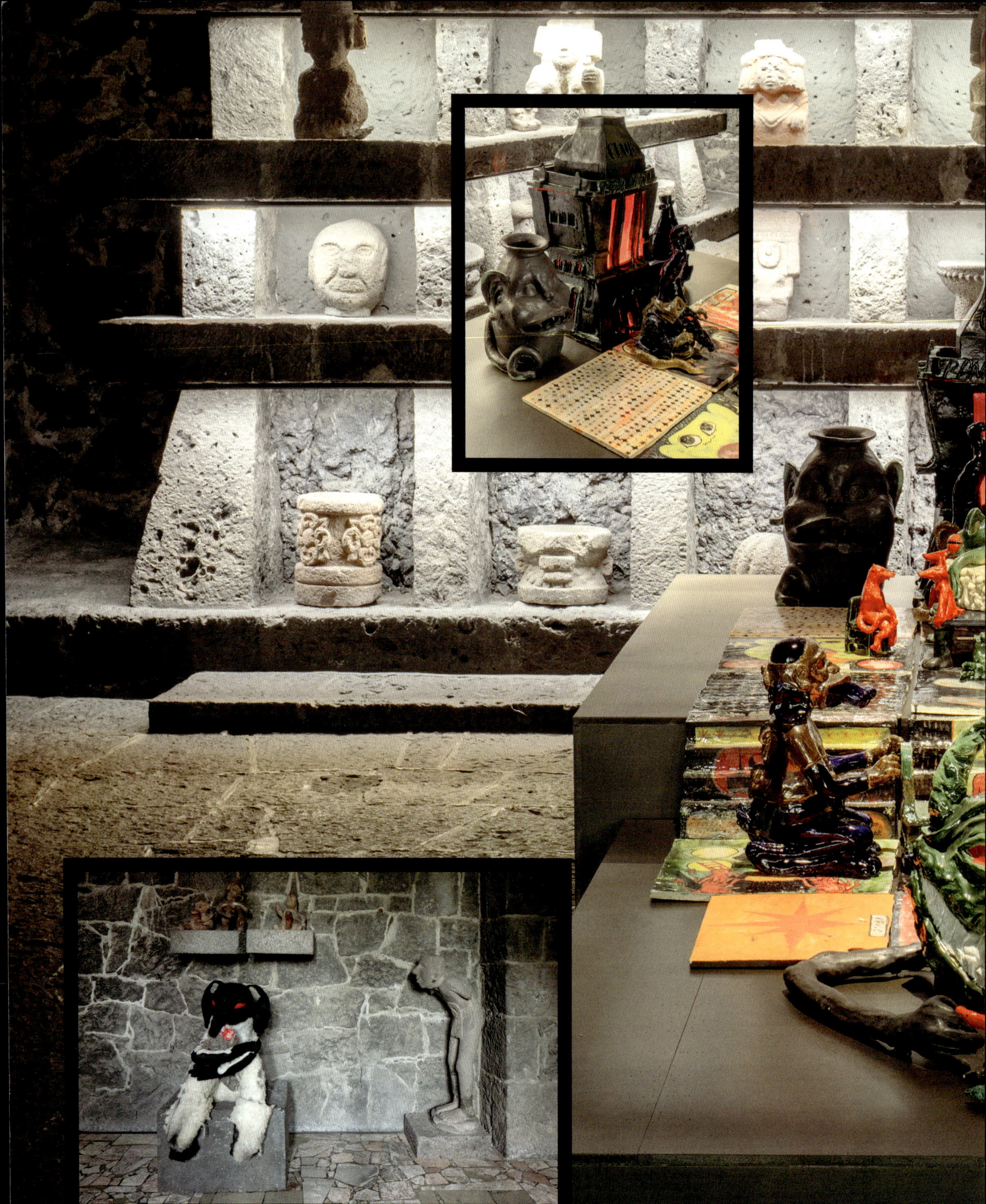

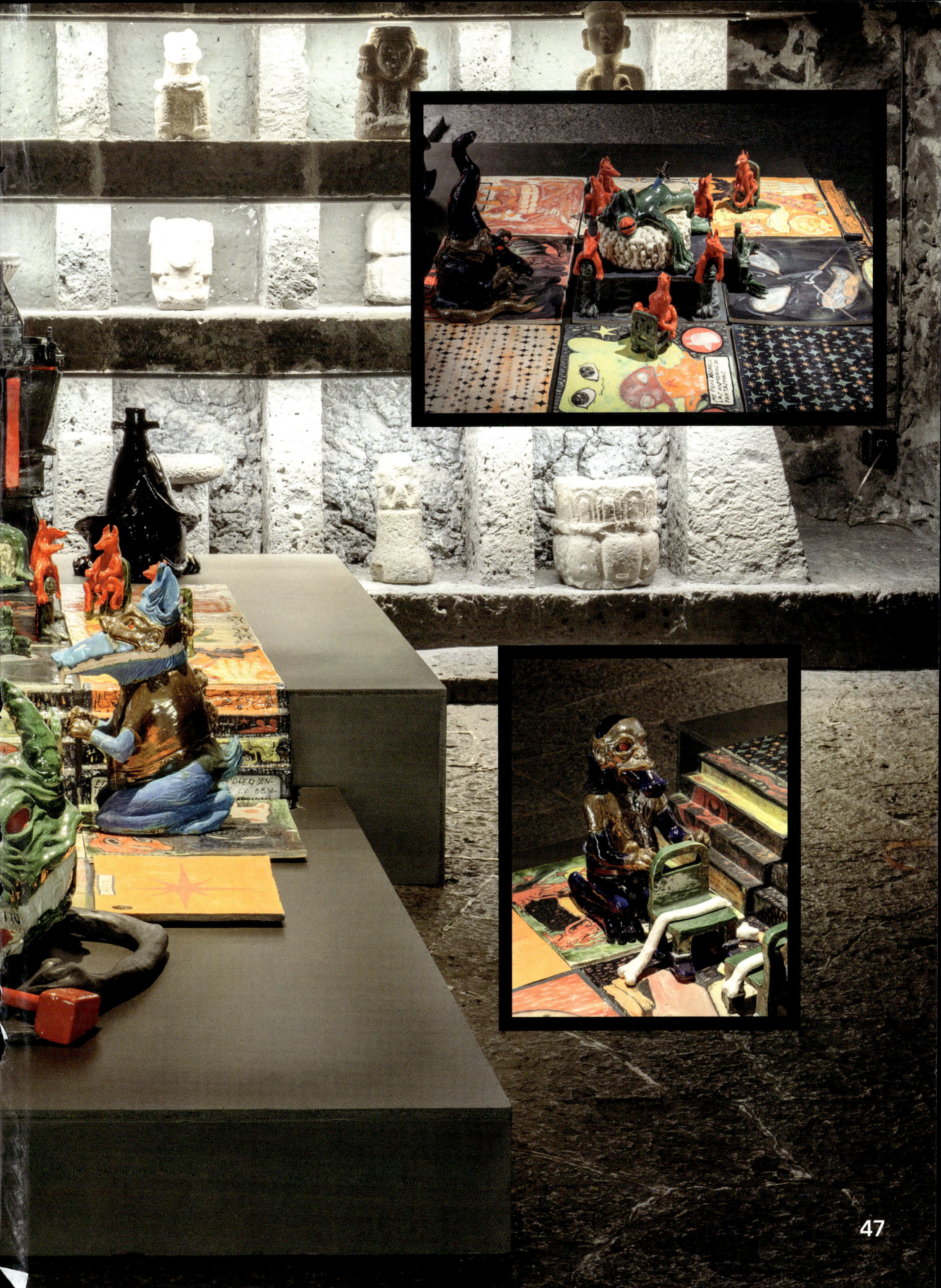

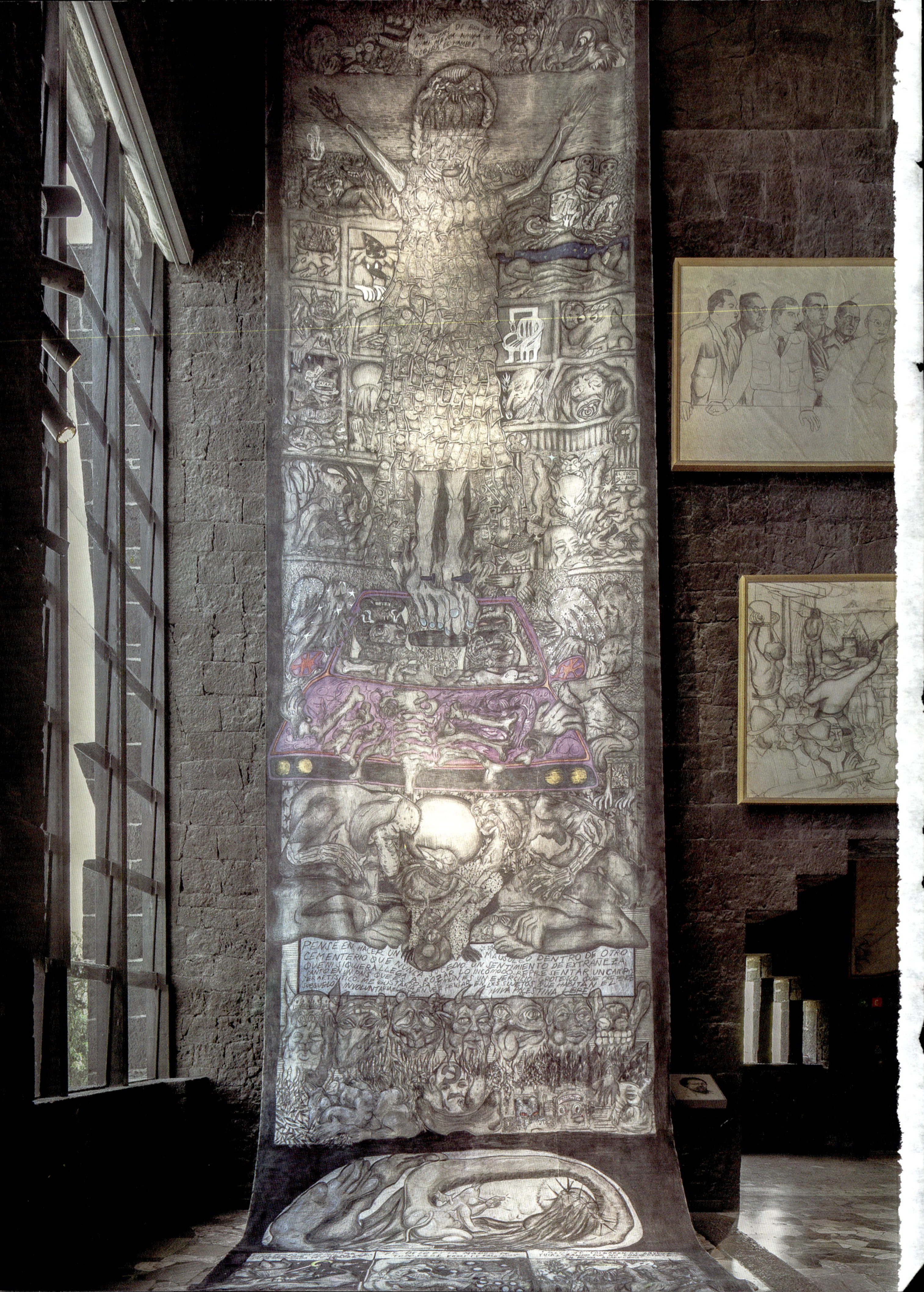